PHILLIP EICHMAN

FROM THE
MOUNTAINSIDE

TIMELESS TRUTHS FROM THE
SERMON ON THE MOUNT

21st CENTURY CHRISTIAN

From the Mountainside
ISBN: 978-0-89098-955-5

©2025 by 21st Century Christian, Inc
Nashville, TN 37215
All rights reserved.

Unless otherwise noted, Scripture quotations are taken from the are taken from The Holy Bible, New International Version®, NIV®. Copyright ©1973, 1978, 1984, 2011 by Biblica, Inc. Used with permission of Zondervan. All rights reserved worldwide. www.zondervan.com

Scripture quotations marked (CEV) are taken from the Contemporary English Version. Contemporary English Version® Copyright ©1995 American Bible Society. All rights reserved.

Scripture quotations marked (IEB) are taken from the International English™ Bible. Copyright ©1978, 2014, 2022 by International Bible Translators, Inc. All rights reserved.

Scripture quotations marked (NLT) are taken from the New Living Translation. Holy Bible, New Living Translation, copyright ©1996, 2004, 2015 by Tyndale House Foundation. Used by permission of Tyndale House Publishers, Inc., Carol Stream, Illinois 60188. All rights reserved.

Cover design by Jared Kendall

Table of Contents

Introduction
Matthew 5—7

We often think of Jesus as Lord, Savior, or Son of God, but one of the names or titles used most often for Jesus was "teacher." Jesus spent much of His time teaching others about God and His kingdom. He taught people along the road as they traveled, in private homes, in synagogues, and in the temple.

Sometimes, He taught individuals one on one. At other times, He taught groups of people and large audiences. Jesus has often been referred to as a "master teacher" because of His different teaching styles and techniques to reach people at various levels of understanding and/or status.

One of the largest collections of Jesus' teachings is found in the Sermon on the Mount in Matthew 5–7.[1] Some of Jesus' words recorded in the Sermon on the Mount are comforting, others are surprising or even shocking, but for the followers of Jesus, every single word is important.

The Sermon on the Mount is a description of what the followers of Jesus are to be like. A key word for understanding the Sermon on the Mount is *different*. As author John Stott once pointed out, *"Jesus emphasized that his true followers, the citizens of God's kingdom, were to be different from others."*[2]

The Sermon on the Mount seems to be quite demanding. Can we live up to the standards of the Sermon on the Mount? No. It is too stringent and too difficult to follow completely. In fact, some people are turned away from the Sermon on the Mount because it is so exacting. What then is the Sermon on the Mount and why did Jesus teach this if it is so difficult to follow? Some have called it God's "ideal" for those who are in His kingdom. It is a goal toward which each follower of Jesus should be moving. The Sermon on the Mount is the standard or ideal of discipleship for all Christians. As we become more and more like the "ideal disciple," we will also become more and more like Jesus because the life that He followed is the life described in the Sermon on the Mount.

People have always had an interest in the Sermon on the Mount. With such a wide variety and amount of materials that have been written, you might think

---

1.   A section of similar teaching, sometimes called the Sermon on the Plain from the reference to "a level place" in verse 17, is found in Luke 6:17–49. It may be that Jesus taught similar material on more than one occasion, or it may be that these are two accounts of the same event. We do not know for sure.

2.   John R. W. Stott, *The Message of the Sermon on the Mount* (Downers Grove, IL: Inter-Varsity Press, 1987), 18.

that we would know just about everything there is to know about the Sermon on the Mount. Each time that you read it, however, you will find some new insight or something new that you had not seen before.

Centuries have passed since Jesus first taught these lessons, and we might think that it's outdated. As we begin to study, we will see that the message of Jesus recorded in the Sermon on the Mount is just as relevant and meaningful for us today as it was for those who first heard it.

We are
to show
mercy
to *everyone.*

One

Blessings for Your Journey

The Beatitudes
Matthew 5:1–12

The Sermon on the Mount begins with a series of statements known as the Beatitudes. This title comes from *beatus*, the Latin translation of the Greek word for "blessed" or "happy." The word *blessed* is common in the Bible, especially in the Psalms and Book of Proverbs.[1] Those who first heard Jesus teach the Beatitudes would have been familiar with this style of proverbial sayings.

The Beatitudes are concerned with discipleship and how to live in obedience and devotion to God. The Beatitudes were not intended for only the spiritual elite, but are characteristics or qualities that all Christians

---

1. For some examples see Psalm 1:1; Proverbs 3:13; Matthew 11:6; Acts 20:35; and Revelation 1:3.

should develop. The Beatitudes, like the rest of the Sermon on the Mount, are not just a collection of moral teachings, but rather a description of the radical demands of Jesus for those who follow Him.

The key word in each of the Beatitudes is *blessed*. We see this in each of the Beatitudes, which begin with "Blessed are the…" This word means "blessed," but it can also mean "happy," "fortunate," or "favored." Most English versions translate the word as "blessed," while a few such as Phillips and the Good News Translation translate the word as "happy."

Each Beatitude also has the idea of a "blessing" or something that is given by God. There are eight qualities or characteristics described, and eight blessings promised by God. Are these blessings in the present or in the future? Some are blessings that come to those who are now living the Christian life, and others are blessings that will come in the future as a reward in heaven.

Earlier in Matthew's account, we see the first recorded teaching of Jesus. His words were simple: *"Repent… for the kingdom of heaven is near"* (Matthew 4:17, NLT). In the Sermon on the Mount, Jesus began to describe or define the traits or characteristics of those who belong to that kingdom.

There is a traditional site for the Sermon on the Mount, but the actual location is not known. It was probably near the town of Capernaum on a hillside leading down to the Sea of Galilee that acted as a natural amphitheater. Verses 1–2 explain the setting. A large number of people had gathered to hear Jesus, and He sat down to teach them. This was the typical manner in which a Jewish rabbi would teach his disciples.

When we look at the Beatitudes, the first thing we notice is a pattern or formula that is repeated in each one. This begins with the word *blessed*, that state of happiness and contentment that comes from being a follower of Jesus. Next, there is a trait or characteristic of the disciple that Jesus was emphasizing. Finally, there is a promise of a reward for those who follow Jesus and develop this trait in their lives. The first Beatitude, for example, consists of these three parts: blessed + poor in spirit + will receive the kingdom of heaven. This same pattern is then repeated for each Beatitude.

Now let's take a look at each of the Beatitudes, noticing in particular the characteristic that Jesus emphasized.

Blessed are the poor in spirit (5:3)

This first Beatitude must have come as a shock because poverty was not and is not considered a "blessing." The word translated as "poor" refers to extreme poverty or complete destitution. The word is sometimes translated as "beggar," someone who has absolutely nothing and must depend upon others for survival. Jesus, however, was speaking of spiritual poverty. To be "poor in spirit" is to be totally dependent upon God.

William Barclay has commented that one who is "poor in spirit" has *"realized that things mean nothing and that God means everything."*[2] Such persons realize their spiritual needs and the powerlessness that they have without God. They will have learned to trust in God alone and have found joy in doing so.

For those who are "poor in spirit," Jesus has promised the kingdom of heaven. The "kingdom," the "kingdom of God," and the "kingdom of heaven" all refer essentially to the same thing. The Jewish people had been waiting for the

---

2.　William Barclay, *The Gospel of Matthew Volume 1* (Louisville: Westminster John Knox Press, 1975), 92.

Messiah to bring a new kingdom, but they had the wrong idea. Jesus' kingdom is not an earthly kingdom. It is a realm in which God reigns over the hearts and lives of His people.

Blessed are those who mourn (5:4)

Blessedness in mourning was certainly not expected either. Those who mourn are usually seen as unfortunate people to be pitied and comforted. Matthew used the strongest Greek word for mourning that is typically used to describe mourning for the loss of a loved one. Jesus' words could be interpreted literally. God can give healing to those who mourn because of grief or loss. Jesus was likely speaking, however, more in a spiritual sense of mourning for our own sins or the evil, suffering, and sadness that we see in the world.

Perhaps we can envision this type of mourning from one example of Jesus Himself. When He went to the tomb of His friend, Lazarus, Jesus knew that He had the power to raise Lazarus from the dead, but He was still deeply moved by the sadness of the occasion and grief experienced by His friends, and He wept.

To those who mourn, Jesus promised comfort. This is a concept that is found elsewhere in Scripture as well (Psalm 23:4; 119:50,76; Isaiah 49:13; 2 Corinthians 1:3).

Blessed are the meek (5:5)

The word *meek* does not mean weak, but rather gentle, humble, or self-controlled. It is the realization of one's dependence upon God. Jesus used the word to describe Himself when He said, *"I am gentle [or "meek"] and humble in heart"* (Matthew 11:29, NIV).

The opposite of *meek* is a person who is aggressive, selfish, and domineering. This is an example of a paradox in Jesus' teaching. It is easy to see that the ones who seem to succeed in life are not those who are "meek" or "gentle," but rather the opposite. It would seem then that the promise to "inherit the earth" is more in the next life in the future than in the present.

Blessed are those who hunger and thirst for righteousness (5:6)

Jesus used a powerful image here. Hunger and thirst are two physiological processes that were real to people living in Jesus' day. Jesus was looking, however, beyond physical hunger and thirst. The image that Jesus used was of a spiritual longing for righteousness that is comparable to extreme thirst and hunger. In other words, seeking righteousness should be a high priority that characterizes the lives of the followers of Jesus.

Blessed are the merciful (5:7)

The background for this Beatitude comes from the Hebrew word *hesed* that is translated as "loving kindness" or "steadfast love." This described the "mercy" that God showed to His people, even when they did not obey Him.

Jesus did not specify to whom His disciples are to show mercy. He did not need to do so. We are to show mercy to everyone. This becomes much more apparent later on in the Sermon on the Mount and in other places where Jesus emphasized that only those who show mercy and forgiveness to others will receive mercy and forgiveness themselves.

Blessed are the pure in heart (5:8)

Jesus' promise for the "pure in heart" to see God likely refers to the next life rather than the present. Jesus was using the "heart" here as the center of feelings and emotions. A person with a pure heart will be centered on God instead of Satan and evil. That is not to say that such a person would never sin, but that their life will be under God's rule, and Satan and sin will no longer be their master.

Blessed are the peacemakers (5:9)

The basis for this Beatitude is in the Hebrew word for "peace," or *shalom*, which means much more than the absence of conflict. *Shalom* can mean "completeness" and "well-being" as well as "peace." It is a mindset and way of living and thinking that is free of strife, anger, and discord.

A peacemaker is the opposite of a troublemaker. A peacemaker tries to bring reconciliation, but a trouble-maker stirs things up and drives people apart. Jesus' promised reward for the peacemakers is impressive. They are to be *"called sons [or "children"] of God."*

Blessed are those who are persecuted (5:10–12)

This Beatitude is perhaps the most unexpected of all. No one likes to be abused or harmed in any way. And even though we may try to live in peace with everyone, there may still be those who oppose or even persecute us.

Jesus was not referring to simply being mistreated or misunderstood. He was talking about suffering in God's service. History is filled with examples of those who suffered and even died for their faith. Once again, Jesus' statement is paradoxical — when you are persecuted, Jesus said to *"rejoice and be glad."*

From this brief look at the Beatitudes, we can see that Jesus demands a way of life that is radically different from the culture of His time or of any time. Yet, Jesus was entirely open and upfront with His message. Nothing was hidden or held back. Being a follower of Jesus may be the most difficult thing that a person can do, but the blessings and rewards for such a life are greater than anyone can imagine.

PEAK REFLECTIONS

1. Which of the Beatitudes refer to our relationship with God and which ones refer to our relationship with other people?
2. Of the promised blessings, which ones are part of this present life and which ones will come in eternity?
3. How do the Beatitudes contrast with everyday life?
4. What is a *paradox*? Which of the Beatitudes seem to be the most paradoxical?
5. How do you think that those who first heard Jesus felt about the Beatitudes? Is the same true of us today?

Each day
that we live,
our *lives* are
to be a **light**
to *others*.

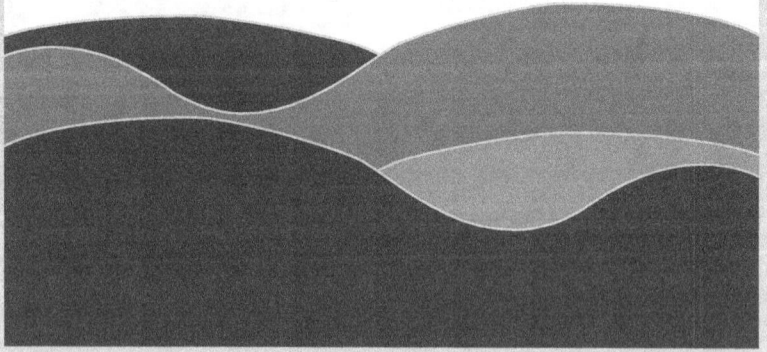

Two

Zest for the Ascent

Salt and Light
Matthew 5:13–16

Most of the people living in our country today are literate, but in Jesus' time, things were different. Few people could read and write, and writing materials were expensive for those who could read and write. In that culture, information was communicated mainly by word of mouth through stories and sayings that could be easily remembered.

Jesus was a master teacher and used stories, parables, and figures of speech in His teaching. In these verses from the Sermon on the Mount, Jesus used a type of figure of speech called a *metaphor*.

The most commonly used figures of speech are the simile and the metaphor. A simile is a comparison that uses "like" or "as." Jesus' words, *"I am sending you out like sheep among wolves,"* is an example of a simile (Matthew 10:16). A metaphor is also a comparison, but does not have a connecting word ("like" or "as") as in a simile.

"You are the salt of the earth..." and *"You are the light of the world..."* are metaphors. Jesus did not mean literally salt or light, but rather used the words figuratively. He used these figures of speech to compare the Christian life with something that His listeners understood: salt and light. He also left them with a mental picture so that they would not soon forget what He had taught them.

Like any of Jesus' teaching, and all of the Bible for that matter, these two examples are set within the culture of the time. For this reason, we need to consider the context and understand the history behind Jesus' words. Once we understand what Jesus was teaching those first-century listeners, then we can begin to see how to apply the teachings to us today.

"You are the salt of the earth"

Today, we tend to take salt for granted. It is always there on the table or in the kitchen cabinet. Unless we have some health issue that is related to salt intake, we don't think much about salt. Sodium chloride is its chemical name, but we just call it table salt.

It was a little different in Jesus' day. Salt was highly valued in the ancient world. The Greeks thought that salt was divine and associated it with the gods. The Romans used salt almost like money. Soldiers were sometimes paid in salt, and our word *salary* comes from the Latin word for *salt*. So when Jesus spoke of salt, it would have caught His listeners' attention.

What did Jesus mean when He said, *"You are the salt of the earth"* (Matthew 5:13)? Salt was used in several ways at that time. First of all, salt was associated with purity. Salt was frequently used as an offering to pagan gods. Under the Law of Moses, certain types of Jewish sacrifices were also offered with salt. If we as Christians are going to be the salt of the earth, then we must be examples of purity in our lives.

Salt was also used, and still is used in certain instances, to preserve fish and meat, and also has cleansing and antiseptic properties. If Christians are to be "the salt of the earth," then we must also have the qualities of cleansing and preserving. Wherever we find ourselves, we should be making it a better place by the cleansing and preserving nature of our behavior. Whether it is at work, at school, at the grocery, or anywhere else, our lives should be like "salt."

Probably, the most familiar use of salt is to give flavor to food. If you don't believe me, try a salt-free diet for a while. Many people see Christianity as totally negative and taking all the "flavor" out of life. We need to show people that you can have a good time and still be a Christian. Salt is not bitter, and neither should our lives be bitter. Instead, the lives of the followers of Jesus should have a Christ-like flavor that is apparent to those around them.

Jesus also spoke about salt that had lost its "saltiness." Many explanations have been given to help understand this statement. Pure salt is chemically made up of sodium chloride and cannot be made less salty. When we go to the grocery store, we see all kinds of salt: iodized salt, salt without iodine, sea salt, Kosher salt, low-sodium salt, even salt substitutes for those on special diets. In Bible times, salt came from the Dead Sea or salt marshes and was often filled with impurities and could at times be almost tasteless. That seems to be what Jesus was talking about.

Jesus' point was that "un-salty" salt is worthless. In a similar way, a Christian who is not the "salt of the earth" is not worth much to Jesus. If we do not have these purifying, preserving, and flavoring qualities in our lives, then something is wrong.

We don't want to go too far in the other direction either. We don't want to become so "salty" that we drive people away rather than attract them to Jesus.

"You are the light of the world"

Light is an important theme in the Bible, especially as it contrasts with darkness. Light is used at times in the Old Testament to personify God, especially in the Psalms (Psalm 27:1; 76:4; 78:14). God appeared to Moses in a burning bush and led the children of Israel in the wilderness by a pillar of fire at night.

Light is an important topic in the New Testament as well. In 1 John, we read *"God is light"* and that Christians are to walk in that light (1 John 1:5–7). In the Gospel of John, Jesus is described as the light that has come into the world (John 1:4–9). In John 8:12 and 9:5 Jesus said, *"I am the light of the world."*

Here in the Sermon on the Mount, Jesus says that His disciples are also to be "the light of the world." That is a great compliment, but also a great responsibility. We might dismiss it as a children's song, but there is a lot of what Jesus was talking about in the words of the song "This Little Light of Mine."

To illustrate His meaning, Jesus used some examples. Jesus' first example was a city on a hill. Perhaps Jesus was alluding to Jerusalem. It was described as the *"light to the nations"* in the Old Testament. Also, Jerusalem was built on top of a hill with an elevation of about 2,500 feet and can be seen for miles around. Jesus' point was that you can't hide a city on a hill. It is there for everyone to see.

Jesus' second example was a lamp. In the ancient world, it was quite dark when the sun went down, and a small lamp was the only source of light for the common people. This was likely an oil lamp that was made of simply a small bowl and a wick. They did not give much light, but it was usually all that they had.

Light is meant to be seen. You do not hide a light; you put it where it can provide illumination. In a similar way, we are to show our "Christian light" to others. Our language and behavior, the way we think and act, should be like a light to others. If you are a Christian, then others will be watching. Some may watch hoping to see you fail, but others may be watching because they see something valuable and important in your life. If Christians act differently on Sunday than the rest of the week, then something is wrong with their lives and their light. Each day that we live, our lives are to be a light to others. This is not to bring glory to us, but to God.

Writer Haddon Robinson summed up this passage well: *"... God needs our light where the world is darkest. The blacker the night the greater the need for a light bulb. If a bulb does not shine, it's not because of the darkness. Darkness cannot put out light... Darkness gets darker because the light fails. When we fail to reflect Christ's light we let darkness win."*[1]

---

1. Haddon W. Robinson, *The Christian Salt and Light Company: A Contemporary Study of the Sermon on the Mount* (Grand Rapids: Discovery House Publishers, 1988), 106.

Robinson went on to conclude, *"Jesus did not call us to be magnificent chandeliers for people to admire. He called us to make a difference in the darkness."*[2]

Jesus' figurative use of salt and light illustrates that Christians are to be different. Different, that is, in a good way that attracts people to Jesus rather than turning them away. Various commentators have pointed out that in the original language, there is an emphasis that we do not see in English. In a sense, Jesus was saying His disciples are the *only* salt and the *only* light in the world. As Christians, we need for our lives to have the preserving, flavoring effects of salt and the illuminating property of light.

PEAK REFLECTIONS

1. In the Beatitudes, Jesus spoke of certain characteristics or traits of His disciples, such as "poor in spirit," "meek," and being a "peacemaker." How do these relate to His teaching on salt and light in these verses?
2. Why did Jesus frequently use figurative language like these examples?
3. Why is Jesus' use of figurative language still compelling for us today?
4. How do these two examples illustrate the need to pay attention to the historical and cultural context of teachings in the Bible?
5. How can we be salt and light to those around us without becoming offensive to others?

---

2. Haddon W. Robinson, *The Christian Salt and Light Company*, 106.

To Jesus,
feelings, emotions,
and *attitudes* are
just as important
as the **actions**
themselves.

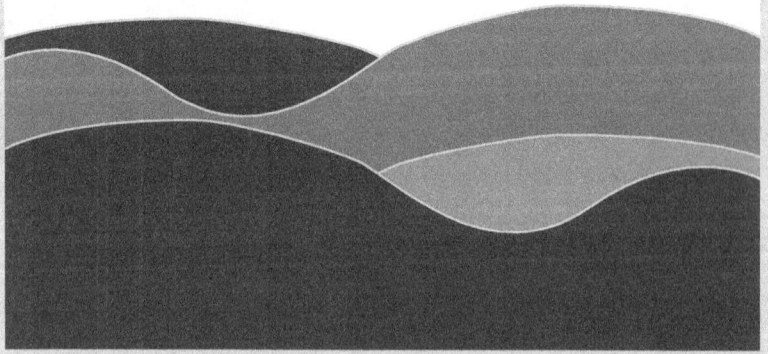

Three

Foundation
in the Foothills

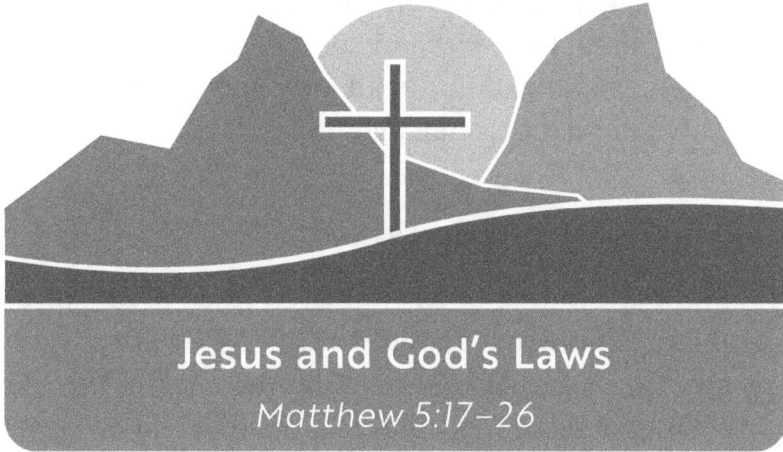

Jesus and God's Laws
Matthew 5:17–26

Jesus was Jewish. He was born into a Jewish family and lived in a community and culture that was Jewish. The people who first heard the teachings of Jesus were also Jewish. Everything, not just their religion, but every aspect of their daily lives was somehow related and centered in the Old Testament Law or Law of Moses. The teaching of the Jewish rabbis of the time was from the Law of Moses, and we might assume that Jesus' teachings would be similar. As we delve deeper into the Sermon on the Mount, however, we will see that this was not the case.

In the previous lessons from the Sermon on the Mount, we saw that the key word for understanding Jesus' teaching is *different*. This is going to become more apparent as we continue our study, especially in this lesson where Jesus' teaching centers on the Law of Moses. We are going to be looking at two passages. In the first passage, Jesus explained His relationship with the Old Testament. In the second, we will see an example of how Jesus expanded and made the commandments of the Law more comprehensive.

Obeying God's laws (5:17–20)

From the beginning of His ministry, Jesus used expressions like *"I say to you..."* and *"I tell you..."* These were phrases that indicated authority. The rabbis did not teach in this way. They would always refer to either the Law of Moses or to some previous rabbi to establish their authority. Jesus' use of authority in His teaching would have come as a surprise. In Mark's Gospel, we read that the people were amazed by Jesus' authority (Mark 1:27). Because Jesus spoke with such authority, some of His listeners must have wondered how He looked at the Law of Moses.

As Jesus stated here in the Sermon on the Mount, He did not come to abolish the law. Instead, Jesus came to fulfill the law and to complete God's plan for redeeming mankind. We see this in the Old Testament prophecies that Jesus fulfilled, especially those regarding the Messiah (Luke 24:44–49). Jesus was also the fulfillment of the Old Testament system of sacrifice. For centuries, the Jewish people had sacrificed animals — day after day, week after week, and year after year. Thousands of animals had been sacrificed, and all of them pointed toward a final sacrifice that would bring complete atonement for sins. Remember John the Baptist's words: *"Look, the Lamb of God, who takes away the sin of the world!"* (John 1:29). Numerous other statements in the New Testament affirm that Jesus' sacrifice accomplished this (Romans 6:10; Hebrews 10:1–11).

The death of Jesus on the cross brought into existence a new law or new covenant. Paul wrote that *"Christ is the end of the law"* (Romans 10:4, NASB). That does not mean, however, that we do not need to obey God's law. In verses 18–19 Jesus made clear His attitude toward the law. Jesus also noted the continuance of God's law. Even though there is a new covenant, it is still God's covenant.

Some elements of the Old Testament law did come to an end at the cross. This includes the sacrifices and priesthood, for example. The Sabbath, as a special day, was also replaced as the day of worship by the first day of the week for Christians to worship.

Jesus' comment in verse 20 about surpassing the righteousness of the Pharisees and teachers of the law must have especially come as a shock. The Pharisees and teachers of the law were the religious leaders and should have been an example. The religious leaders, however, based their "righteousness" on keeping rules and the outward appearance rather than the inner, spiritual aspects of righteousness.

In what follows, Jesus made it plain that to keep the laws outwardly, but break them inwardly is wrong and should not be practiced by Jesus' disciples. To Jesus, feelings, emotions, and attitudes are just as important as the actions themselves.

Jesus' attitude toward the Law of Moses should not be confused with His opposition to the human rules that had been added to the law. These additional regulations had been added on to certain commandments by the religious leaders, especially the Pharisees. In the Gospels, we see several examples of occasions when Jesus was opposed to these "human traditions" (or "traditions of men"). These included, for example, regulations on ceremonial purity (rules regarding clean and unclean), special handwashing practices (Mark 7:1–8), and prohibition of healing a person on the Sabbath (Mark 3:1–6). Jesus respected and faithfully kept the Law of Moses, but He was not concerned about legalistically keeping the tedious rules that had been added to God's laws.

Jesus' first example of applying God's laws (5:21–26)

Here in Matthew 5, we see examples of Jesus' teaching that show us that God's laws are more than just rule-keeping. The first of these deals with the command not to commit murder. Willful killing of another person, or murder, was prohibited in the Ten Commandments (Exodus 20:13) and carried a death penalty (Exodus 21:12–14; Leviticus 24:21). In addition to the actual act of murder, Jesus added that anyone who is angry is also subject to judgment (vv. 21–22).

Jesus began by saying, *"You have heard it said... But I tell you..."* This was a formula that Jesus used in several of His illustrations. Jesus' listeners knew the commandments, but they would not have been ready for what followed. In each case, Jesus spoke with authority and went far beyond their understanding of what the commandments meant.

In this first example, Jesus said that anger toward another person can be as serious as taking the person's life. Everyone is angry at times, but Jesus was speaking of anger that sought harm to another person or some sort of revenge.

Jesus also spoke of name-calling and using words like *raca* ("stupid," "empty-headed," or "idiot") and "fool" that meant not just "stupid," but morally and spiritually corrupt. Jesus was not just talking about joking or kidding; He was talking about a hate-filled put-down expressed in anger. These were abusive words of contempt intended to be insulting and hurtful. Murder is a terrible wrong, but so are anger, hatred, and a desire to harm others. Some may feel that Jesus is somewhat extreme in this matter. His point is, however, that when a person is angry enough to speak to another person in this way, it is wrong and may lead to further conflict.

Anger can certainly lead to further conflict, but not all anger is wrong. Jesus Himself became angry at times. Anger against sin or injustice, for example, is not wrong, as long as it is not directed at the person. We should be angry with someone who produces pornography, sells drugs, or abuses another person, but we should not attack them personally. As the saying goes, "Hate the sin, love the sinner."

In verses 23–26 Jesus went on to give specific examples of situations that can lead to anger and ill feelings toward others. His emphasis seems to be not letting the situation reach the point of anger, but rather to be reconciled with the other person.

Jesus used two examples to illustrate how damaged relationships caused by anger and ill feelings must be repaired. The first of these is an example in the context of worship. Not allowing grudges and disagreements to keep you from serving God was His first point. To help understand this example, we can just paraphrase it in modern language: "If you are going into the auditorium to worship and remember that there is a problem between you and someone else, then go to the person and make it right."

Next, Jesus said to settle disagreements quickly. This second example comes from a Gentile legal context, but the point is the same. We should settle differences quickly before they become a more serious problem.

Jesus used these examples to show that we need to do whatever we can to restore relationships and bring about reconciliation. Whenever we know that something is wrong, we need to take care of it rather than letting it fester. Anger, grudges, bad feelings toward others — these are all wrong, just as wrong as taking another person's life. There are no small sins, and whenever we realize that we have done wrong, we need to make it right. First, we need to make it right with God and then with any other persons who may have been affected by our actions.

Such radical views must have caused some of Jesus' listeners to question His teachings, especially concerning the Law of Moses. Jesus made it clear that He did not propose to *abolish* the law. Instead, He came into our world to fulfill the old law. In doing so, He also gave us a new law. Some may say that the New Testament is based upon grace and there is no need to obey any laws. From what we see in the Sermon on the Mount, however, we must conclude that such a view is incorrect and that Jesus did leave His followers with definite rules for conducting their lives.

PEAK REFLECTIONS

1. Why was it important for Jesus to explain His relationship with the Law of Moses?
2. How was Jesus' teaching different from other Jewish rabbis?
3. What is the significance of Jesus' statement in verse 20?
4. What is the difference between the commandment about murder in the Law of Moses and Jesus' new expression of the commandment?
5. What did Jesus say about disagreements with others? How should they be handled?

Jesus went beyond the physical *action*... to what occurs in the **heart**.

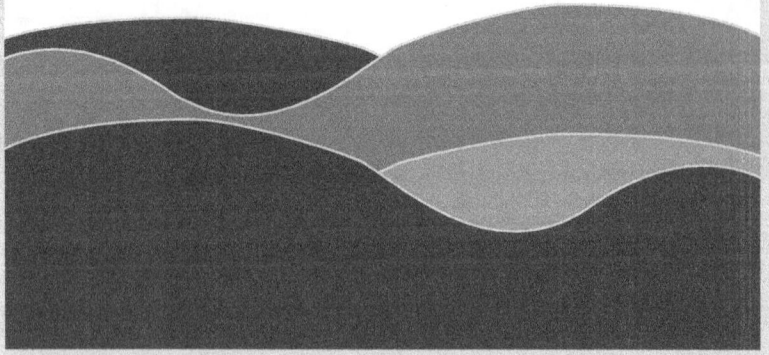

Four

Uphill Struggles

Sexual Sins, Divorce, Oaths
Matthew 5:27-37

As we continue our study in the Sermon on the Mount, we again see how Jesus' words would have amazed, surprised, and even shocked those in His audience. This was especially true of Jesus' comments on the Old Testament commandments. Those who heard Him had grown up with a particular understanding of these commandments, then Jesus came along and turned their understanding upside down with a new way of thinking about the commandments.

Adultery and lust (5:27–30)

After dealing with murder and hate, Jesus then turned to adultery. *"You shall not commit adultery"* was the seventh commandment of the Ten Commandments given to Moses by God on Mount Sinai.

Adultery is a sin involving sexual relations with someone who is not the person's spouse. The fact that God placed a prohibition against adultery in the Ten Commandments, the 10 statements that summarize the law, indicates that God sees this as a grievous sin. It is a commandment that was meant to provide stability for marriage, the family, and the community.

Joseph's words to Potiphar's wife indicate that adultery was considered a sin long before the giving of the Law of Moses (Genesis 39:9). Condemnation of adultery has been found in other ancient law codes as well. The severe death penalty in Israel, however, is somewhat unique (Leviticus 20:10; Deuteronomy 22:22).

In verse 28, Jesus added to the commandment against adultery that *"anyone who looks at a woman lustfully has already committed adultery with her in his heart"* (NIV). There are two key words here in Jesus' addition to the commandment: *lustfully* and *heart*. The original word translated as *lust* means "to long for, to covet, or to lust after." It describes any type of strong desire and is used both in a positive and negative sense in the New Testament. It is used positively in the sense of wanting or desiring something and is translated as "longing" or "desire" (Luke 15:16; 16:21; Philippians 1:23; 1 Thessalonians 2:17). More frequently, the word is used in a negative sense, as Jesus did in this instance.

God created human beings with a desire for the opposite sex. Jesus was not speaking of the natural attraction of a man and woman, however. He was speaking of an intentional, deliberate, lustful desire and longing to have sexual relations with someone who is not your spouse. As he had done before with murder and hatred, Jesus went beyond the physical action condemned by the commandment of the law to what occurs in the heart, the center of emotions and will. In other words, lustful desire is just as wrong as actual illicit sexual relations.

Jesus' teaching here is in terms of a man lusting after a woman, but this is not limited to men only. It is more common in men because they are more visually attracted, but is not restricted to only men. Women, too, can have similar emotions and desires. It is something for all followers of Jesus to be aware and avoid if possible.

To illustrate the seriousness of such improper desires, Jesus used some strong language in verses 29–30. What He said here is not to be taken literally. He was using what is called *hyperbolic language* to emphasize His point. A hyperbole is a figure of speech that uses exaggeration for emphasis. A mother may say to her child, "I have told you a thousand times not to do that to your brother." Obviously, she had not said it 1,000 times. It was a hyperbole.

Jesus used hyperboles on other occasions as well. One example is Jesus' describing a person with a beam sticking out of his eye (Matthew 7:3–4). Another example is when Jesus said, *"... it is easier for a camel to go through the eye of a needle than for a rich person to enter the kingdom of God"* (Matthew 19:24, ESV).

Jesus obviously did not literally mean for you to gouge out your eye or cut off your hand. After all, a person who is blind or has only one hand can still have lustful desires. The seriousness of these hyperbolic examples, however, shows us the importance of not allowing sins, like lust, to be a part of our lives.

Divorce (5:31–32)

From adultery and lust, Jesus moved then to some brief comments on divorce. Marriage and divorce are serious matters, but many people today do not take them seriously, leading to so many marriages and families being broken up by divorce. The same was true in the first century when Jesus first spoke these words. Divorce was common in the Greek and Roman cultures. Sadly, it was also not uncommon among the Jewish people.

Among the Jewish people, marriage and divorce were handled within the family. There were no legal documents such as marriage licenses, and divorce was not a legal proceeding involving a judge and court as it is today.

Since Jesus was still teaching in the context of the Law of Moses, to fully understand what He was talking about, we need to go back to the law itself. The key passage is found in Deuteronomy 24:1–4. This was not a commandment encouraging divorce, but rather a provision in the law to regulate how divorce was to be carried out.

We also need to understand the cultural context within the Jewish community. In Jewish culture, women had few legal rights, and wives were viewed as the property of their husbands. A Jewish man could divorce his wife, but a wife could not divorce her husband. In addition, there was no agreement among the Jewish people on the proper grounds for divorce. Some of their religious teachers believed that divorce should only be allowed on the basis of sexual immorality. Others held that a man could divorce a wife for almost any reason. This disagreement over the proper grounds for divorce had been going on long before the time of Jesus.

For a man to simply force his wife to leave and fend for herself would have been devastating for her. The passage in Deuteronomy 24:1–4 was intended to regulate the process of divorce among the people of Israel. The bill (or certificate) of divorce was to prevent a husband from failing to make some provision for the divorced wife. It was to protect the woman, to provide written proof that she had not merely run away from her husband, and to allow her to legally marry another man.

Regardless of the reason for it, divorce is a potentially painful process that divides the marital partners and breaks up the family. We know from passages like Malachi 2:16 that God does not look favorably on divorce.

Later in the Gospels, Jesus spoke in more detail on divorce (Matthew 19:1–9; Mark 10:1–12). In doing so, Jesus went back to the creation account in Genesis showing that it was God's intent from the beginning that marriage should be one man and one woman for life.

Like much of the Sermon on the Mount, Jesus was describing God's "ideal" for marriage. Sometimes divorce may be necessary, but it still isn't a part of God's original plan for human beings that He created.

Oaths (5:33–37

The immediate application for Jesus' comments on swearing and oaths was for those living at that time, but there are also principles here for us as well. The first thing we need to realize is that when Jesus used the word *swear*, He was not using it in the sense of cursing or using foul language. He was referring to the practice of oaths to validate a person's statement.

Telling the truth in all situations was important to the Jewish people, as it is for us today as well. Liars, hypocrites, and those who would bear false witness are strongly condemned in both the Old Testament and New Testament. Somehow, the use of oaths to guarantee the truthfulness of a statement had become commonly used by the time of Jesus. It was this practice to which Jesus was referring in these verses.

There were references to oaths and vows in the Old Testament (Exodus 22:10–13; Leviticus 19:12; Numbers 30:2). There were also the commandments that prohibited misusing the name of God and giving false witness or testimony against another person (Exodus 20:7,16).

Jesus was referring to the practice of swearing that a promise or statement was true or binding by certain things, such as "heaven," "earth," "Jerusalem," or "my head." So instead of merely promising to do something, for example, a person would say, "By my life I swear that I will..."

William Barclay made some interesting comments about this practice.[1] He points out that the Jewish people were misusing the oaths for their own purposes. They thought of oaths in two categories: frivolous oaths and evasive oaths. Frivolous oaths were made when there was really no need for them. People used them so much that they had just become accustomed to doing so, without giving it any thought.

---

1.   William Barclay, *The Gospel of Matthew Volume 1*, 158–162.

Evasive oaths were of two types. Certain oaths were considered absolutely binding, and others were not. Any oath that contained the name of God was considered absolutely binding. Any other oath was not and could be evaded in some way. They thought that if God's name was not included, then it was permissible to not take the responsibility seriously and find some sort of loophole to avoid it. Jesus said that this type of thinking is all wrong.

God is involved in all aspects of our lives. For this reason, the followers of Jesus should regard themselves as belonging to God and holding any promise as binding. As Jesus concluded, all answers should be either "yes or no." There should not be any need to swear an oath to guarantee the truth. A person's character should make an oath unnecessary.

PEAK REFLECTIONS

1. What is the difference between the natural attraction of a man and woman and lust?
2. What are some things in our society that can contribute to lust? How can a person avoid them?
3. Thinking of the Sermon on the Mount as a description of God's "ideals," what was His original plan for marriage?
4. What type of oaths was Jesus talking about? Why had they become a problem?
5. How did Jesus say that one of His disciples should answer questions? What does this indicate about a person's character?

Jesus said
to *love* even
your enemies
and to *pray*
for **them**.

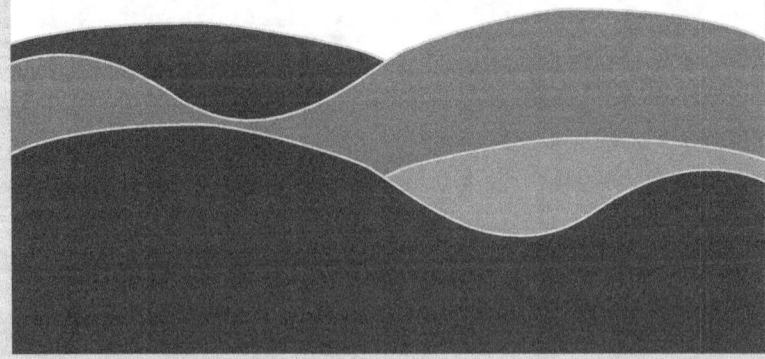

Five

Just Keep Climbing

Turn the Other Cheek, Go the Second Mile, Love Your Enemies
Matthew 5:38-48

E arlier in the Sermon on the Mount Jesus said, "Blessed are the peacemakers, for they will be called sons of God" (Matthew 5:9, NASB). Now He is going to give His disciples opportunities to put that into practice.

"Turn the other cheek," "go the second mile," "love your enemies." These are expressions that many people recognize as coming from the Bible. In this lesson, we will see that these were important points that Jesus made about characteristics of those who are His followers. Are these simple or easy to follow?

No, but no one said that being a follower of Jesus was easy. Living a Christian life can be tough, but with Jesus' example and God's help, we can be successful.

"An eye for an eye" (5:38–42)

Jesus began by saying, *"You have heard that it was said, 'EYE FOR EYE, TOOTH FOR TOOTH.'"* Jesus was referring here to what is known as the law of retaliation or *lex talionis*, which comes from the Latin for "law of retribution."

This law is found three times in the Old Testament (Exodus 21:23–25; Leviticus 24:19–20; Deuteronomy 19:21). Some form of this law is found in other law codes from the ancient world as well, the most well-known being from the Code of Hammurabi, who was a king of Babylon in 18th century B.C.

Some people think that this Old Testament commandment is bloodthirsty and encouraged violence. In reality, the commandment set limits on retaliation and restricted rather than encouraged revenge. In doing so, it helped to prevent feuds and other forms of excessive retribution by attempting to make the punishment fit the crime. It is believed that it was actually rarely carried out among the Jewish people and that monetary settlements served as a substitution for actual physical harm to the guilty person. It also took the punishment away from the individual or family and put it into the hands of a judge.

Here in the Sermon on the Mount, Jesus changed it from a law of limited retaliation to the principle of non-retaliation. In doing so, He prohibited all forms of vengeance against another person.

Instead of an eye for an eye or tooth for tooth, Jesus said, *"Do not resist an evil person."* Jesus was talking about someone who wrongs us, and some translations try to bring out this meaning. The Contemporary English Version, for example, translates this as, *"But I tell you not to try to get even with a person who has done something to you."*

Jesus also gave some examples of non-retaliation. The first of these was to "turn the other cheek." Some people have misunderstood what Jesus meant by this. Jesus was probably not talking about defending yourself against a criminal that has attacked you. He was most likely referring to a backhanded slap that was intended as an insult. This was the meaning of the original Greek word that was used. It is a practice still used today in some cultures as the ultimate form of insult.

We have all experienced someone trying to insult us or hurt is in some other way. Jesus' point seems to be just to ignore it, let it go, and don't try to get back at the person in some way.

Jesus' next example had to do with giving someone the shirt off your back. Some versions translate the words as "tunic" and "cloak." Other versions use "shirt" and "coat." The tunic or shirt was an inner garment, and the cloak or coat was an outer, heavier garment and used also as a blanket at night. Sometimes, these garments were all that a person possessed and may have been used as collateral to borrow money. It is interesting that in the Law of Moses, it was stipulated that the cloak could be taken as a pledge, but must be returned at night (Exodus 22:26–27).

Jesus was saying that if someone wants your tunic, give him your cloak too. In other words, do more than what is required of you.

Jesus' next example was to go the second mile. This comes from an earlier practice in which a soldier could force someone to carry something for him. This continued into the first century, and a Roman soldier could compel a person to carry his pack or baggage for one mile.

If a soldier compelled you to carry his pack, you could comply with the law and do the minimum required. You could even show your contempt and resentment in doing so. Or, you could do more than was required and "go the second mile."

A Roman mile was 1,000 paces. Imagine a first-century Jew being forced to carry a Roman soldier's pack, counting every step of the way, "nine hundred ninety-eight, nine hundred ninety nine, one thousand," and then dropping the pack and walking away in disgust. Then imagine the next day. The same soldier taps another person on the shoulder and demands that he carry his pack. This time it is a Christian, a follower of Jesus. The man picks up the pack and walks down the road. But instead of only carrying it only one mile, he carried it two miles. Doing the unexpected is what Jesus was talking about. It was an example of going beyond what is required

The final examples that Jesus used had to do with sharing your possessions with others. There were commandments in the law concerning loans and giving to the poor (Exodus 22:25; Leviticus 25:35–38; Deuteronomy 23:19–20). There were also examples in the Old Testament that encouraged helping those in need (Proverbs 14:31; 19:17; 21:13). So, what Jesus said here was nothing new, but rather a further reminder of what is expected of His followers.

Love your enemies (5:43–48)

We come now to one of the most demanding tasks that Jesus placed upon His followers: to love your enemies. It is easy to love your family, your friends, and those close to you, but it is much more difficult to love your enemies. Let's just be honest and admit it, some people are not all that loveable. What exactly did Jesus mean? What was He asking us to do?

First of all, we need to look at the commandment that Jesus quoted, *"You have heard that it is said, 'Love your neighbor and hate your enemy.'"* Actually, only a part of this came from the Old Testament: the command to love your neighbor. The part about hating your enemies was probably added by some of the stricter Pharisees. The question they were asking was this: Who is my neighbor? In fact, a man once came to Jesus and asked Him that same question (Luke 10:29). To answer the man, Jesus told the Parable of the Good Samaritan (Luke 10:25–37).

The Pharisees and other religious leaders of the time thought that they had figured it out. Haddon Robinson described it this way: *"They decided where to draw the line. A neighbor was someone close. To those outside their immediate circle they could be indifferent. And there was a whole mass of people that they regarded as enemies and were free to hate. They reasoned that people who weren't their neighbors must be enemies, so they could despise them."*[1]

Instead of this kind of thinking, Jesus said, *"Love your enemies and pray for those who persecute you."* The love that Jesus spoke of is not the same love that we have for a spouse, family member, or friend. It is a different kind of love.

---

1.   Haddon W. Robinson, *The Christian Salt and Light Company*, 174–175.

The Greek word is *agape*. It is sometimes described as undeserved or unmerited love. It is used in the New Testament to describe God's love for us and the kind of love that we are to have for others, even our enemies. It is not an emotional love. It is a thinking, acting love that has also been described as active benevolence. *Agape,* as explained by William Barclay, *"is the power to love those whom we do not like and who may not like us."*[2]

The Old Testament commanded to love your neighbor (Leviticus 19:18). Jesus said to love even your enemies and to pray for them. The only person who could live this out is a Christian — someone who has been forgiven through God's grace and loved by God even when he or she does not deserve it.

Chapter 5 closes with Jesus' words: *"Be perfect, therefore, as your heavenly Father is perfect"* (NIV). The word *perfect* does not mean sinless. It means "mature" or "complete" and is something to work toward.

Jesus' teachings in this passage are once again "ideals" or principles to guide the behavior of those who follow Him. To not pay back the person who hurts you, to show love instead of hate, to help others in need, to love even your enemies, and to go the second mile — these are not the typical behavior that we see in other people. When we begin to do these things, to live like Jesus wants us to live, others will notice that we are different. Not odd, but different in a good way. Remember what Jesus said earlier, *"In the same way, let your light shine before men, that they may see your good deeds and glorify your Father in heaven"* (Matthew 5:16, NIV).

---

2. William Barclay, *The Gospel of Matthew, Volume 1*, 174.

PEAK REFLECTIONS

1. How do we typically respond when someone tries to hurt us? What often happens when we respond this way?
2. What are some ways that we can "go the second mile" today?
3. What happens when you pray for your enemies?
4. How is loving your enemy different from loving a relative or friend?
5. What do you think that Jesus meant when He told us to be "perfect"? Is this perfect as Jesus was perfect, or is it something else?

The followers
of Jesus are
not to draw
attention to
themselves or
seek the **praise**
of others.

Six

A Panoramic Perspective

Having the Right Attitude in Worship and Service to God

Matthew 6:1–8, 16–18

When you give a gift to someone, do you do it to make yourself look good or to show how you feel toward that person? It is really a question of your attitude and motivation, isn't it? If you give the gift to make yourself look good, then your motives are selfish and self-centered. If you give the gift out of love, though, the motive comes from your heart. In a somewhat similar way, Jesus talked about our attitude and motivation in serving and worshiping God.

Don't be a performer (6:1)

Earlier, in Matthew 5:16 Jesus said to *"let your light shine before others, that they may see your good deeds and glorify your Father in heaven."* Here in chapter 6, Jesus was talking about calling attention to ourselves so that others can see how "good" we are, transferring the glory from God to ourselves.

This was a special problem of the religious leaders, and the Pharisees in particular. John, in his Gospel, wrote in that the Pharisees *"loved the praise of men more than the praise of God"* (John 12:42–43, NKJV).

Many people today use websites, blogs, and social media to promote themselves. The religious leaders of Jesus' time may have lacked these, but they had their own ways of promoting and making themselves look good.

Jesus began by saying in verse 1, *"Be careful not to practice your righteousness in front of others to be seen by them. If you do, you will have no reward from your Father in heaven"* (NIV). The word *righteousness* in this verse is also sometimes translated as "good deeds" or "religious duties." These are public demonstrations of devotion to God. Among the Jewish people, there were three: giving to the poor, prayer, and fasting. In the verses that follow, Jesus addressed all three of these, giving guidelines for practicing these religious activities.

Doing good works to be praised by others, to increase your own prestige, or to show others how good you are may appeal to some people, but not to Jesus. The followers of Jesus are not to draw attention to themselves or seek the praise of others, but rather to have the right attitudes and motivation in serving and worshiping God.

Jesus also said that if you do misuse these good works, you will *"have no reward from your Father in heaven."* The key here is the word *reward*. In these few verses, Jesus used the word *reward* seven times — three times in a positive sense and four times in a negative sense. The original word means "a wage or reward" and typically was used to refer to a wage or compensation that was earned. Jesus spoke earlier in Matthew 5:12 of a *"reward in heaven"* for those who endured persecution. All who remain faithful to God and Christ are, in fact, promised an eternal reward (Colossians 3:23–24; Hebrews 11:6). This was the positive sense of a reward from God in which Jesus used the word in verses 4, 6, and 18.

Jesus was pointed in His negative use of the word *reward* (vv. 1, 2, 5, 16). In these verses Jesus was referring to those who sought a "reward" on earth by impressing others with their goodness. They *"have received their reward,"* Jesus said, referring to a reward from others, rather than from God.

Giving to the poor (6:2–4)

Giving to the poor was one of the most important religious duties among the Jewish people. It was also one of the easiest ways to bring glory to yourself. This is what Jesus was condemning: giving for the wrong reason.

Jesus expects His followers to be generous, but generosity is not enough. Once again, Jesus went to the heart of the matter, to the person's motivation. Some people may give to seek the praise of others or to congratulate themselves. They are motivated by selfishness. Jesus wants us instead to give to glorify God and be motivated by love.

"Do not announce it with trumpets," Jesus said (v. 2). There may have been some who did have a fanfare. It seems more likely that Jesus may have just been using irony to describe them, much like our own description of those *"who blow their own horn."*

Jesus called them *hypocrites*, which is another word that Jesus used several times in these verses (vv. 2, 5, 16). Our English words *hypocrite* and *hypocrisy* are derived from the original Greek words. In classical Greek the words did not have a negative meaning. They referred to a speaker, one who recited poetry, or an actor.

The negative sense in which we see these words today began with the Septuagint, the Greek translation of the Old Testament that was completed sometime between the third and second centuries B.C. So, by the time of Jesus, at least among the Jewish people, the words had a definite negative meaning.

In the New Testament, the words are found mainly in the Gospels. There, we see Jesus using the word *hypocrite* in a negative sense to describe those who were like "play-actors," those who were saying one thing and doing another or pretending to be something that they were not. William Barclay made these observations about these words: *"In the [New Testament] there is no sin more strongly condemned than hypocrisy, and in popular opinion there is no sin more universally detested."*[1]

Jesus said, *"They have received their reward in full"* (v. 2). It literally means "paid in full." They had wanted the praise of others, and that was what they received. But there was no reward from God, because their motivation was wrong.

It is easy to be critical of the Pharisees, but we can fall into the same temptation. It is like the man who put

---

1. William Barclay, *New Testament Words* (Louisville: Westminster John Knox, 1964), 140.

a $100 bill in the collection plate, but flashed it around first so that everyone could see it. To prevent things like this Jesus said, "*... do not let your left hand know what your right hand is doing*" (v. 3). This is an interesting illustration on giving that was probably a proverbial saying. Some people have taken this literally. I recall visiting a small church in rural Washington that used a velvet bag for the collection so that you could put your hand inside before releasing your contribution.

Verse 4 is the key to understanding the meaning of Jesus' words. Rather than making a show of it so that everyone will see what we are doing, we should do our giving in secret where only God will know what we are doing.

Praying (6:5–8)

Prayer was also considered an important religious duty by the Jewish people. Some problems had developed, however, which Jesus mentioned. First of all, prayer had become formalized, and the same prayers were being offered time after time. To remedy this, Jesus gave a model prayer in verses 9–15 that we will be looking at in the next lesson. Prayer was also being limited to certain times of the day: morning, afternoon, and evening. The most serious problem, though, was those who prayed to be seen and praised by others. Jesus' point here is to not pray just to impress others, but to pray to God.

The custom at the time was to stop wherever you were at the time of prayer and turn toward the temple and pray. It is thought that some people tried to be in a conspicuous place, like street corners, at the time of prayer so that others could see them pray and praise them for their deep religious conviction.

Jesus did not condemn praying in public, only praying to be seen by others. Instead, Jesus gave us these instructions: pray in private whenever possible and do not babble like the pagans (1 Kings 18:26; Acts 19:34).

Fasting (6:16–18)

Fasting was the third religious act upon which Jesus elaborated. Some of the Jewish people fasted in mourning or as a result of sin. The only day of fasting required by the Old Testament was the Day of Atonement (Leviticus 16:29–34).

In addition, some Jews, such as the Pharisees, fasted regularly two days a week.

Jesus says that some of them went to extremes by putting ashes on their head and face, and maybe even wearing sackcloth to look more pitiful and call attention to themselves. Their motivation was all wrong and once again Jesus used the term *hypocrite* to describe them.

What about us today? There is no command to fast in the New Testament. Some people do it for health reasons and others for religious reasons. If fasting helps you to be closer to God, then fast; but don't do it to just show off or make yourself look holier than others.

Whether it is fasting, praying, or giving, the most important thing to realize is found in Jesus' words *"your Father, who sees what is done in secret, will reward you"* (6:4). We are not to do these things to be seen and praised by others. We are to do them to honor God and as a result, He will reward us for our actions. The rewards from others are only temporary and soon forgotten, but God's rewards are eternal.

PEAK REFLECTIONS

1. What is the difference between "letting your light shine" and showing off?
2. What two kinds of "rewards" was Jesus talking about in these verses? How are they different?
3. How would you describe a hypocrite in your own words? Can you give examples?
4. In what ways is a public prayer different than a private prayer? What aspects of public prayer did Jesus condemn in these verses?
5. What were some reasons for fasting in Bible times? Why might someone fast today? Must all Christians fast to be pleasing to God?

We must
remember that
God knows and
sees **everything**...
He is always
at work for the
good of those
who *love Him*.

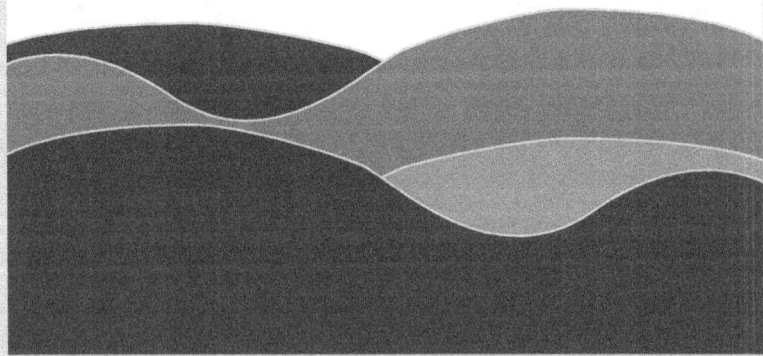

Seven

Reaching the Peak

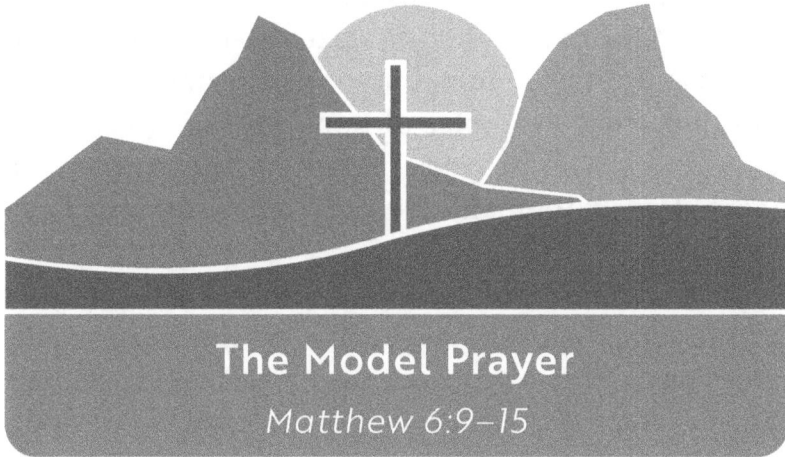

The Model Prayer
Matthew 6:9–15

Prayer is a blessing and gift from God that allows people to communicate with Him. In Matthew 6:5–8 Jesus taught us how *not* to pray; don't be a play-actor praying just to impress others with your religious fervor and don't pray like the pagans with their magic words and babbling repetition. Here in verses 9–13 Jesus gave us an example of what we might call a model prayer. Most people refer to it as the "Lord's prayer." Down through the centuries, many people have memorized and repeated the prayer itself, but what Jesus really gave us is a "framework" from which we can model our own prayers. It is a simple and straightforward prayer, but it is also deeply meaningful.

Jesus' original listeners would have been familiar with prayer. Prayer is common in the Old Testament. Perhaps the first mention of prayer is in Genesis 4:26 where we read about individuals *"calling on the name of the LORD."* There are about a dozen Hebrew words for "pray" and "prayer" found in the Old Testament. There are numerous examples of important Old Testament characters who prayed, including Abraham, Isaac, Jacob, Moses, Hannah, David, Solomon, Jonah, Elisha, and others.

The Old Testament book with the most examples of prayer is Psalms. More than 30 times, prayer is mentioned in some form in the Psalms. These include prayers of praise, thanksgiving, intercession, confession, and lament.

There are several examples of Jesus Himself praying to His Father. These were all associated with significant events in Jesus' life and ministry, and they include Jesus' baptism (Luke 3:21–22), the Transfiguration (Luke 9:28–29), and Jesus' selection of the apostles (Luke 6:12-14). Sometimes, Jesus just went away to be by Himself and to pray (Luke 5:16). There are also the accounts of Jesus' prayer in the Garden of Gethsemane (Matthew 26:36–46) and His lengthy prayer at the end of His ministry recorded in John 17.

It must have been apparent to the disciples that prayer was so important in the life of Jesus. Perhaps this is why in the other account of the "model prayer" in Luke 11:1–4, we read that one of the disciples came to Jesus and requested, *"Lord, teach us to pray."* As we begin to look at the prayer, let us be like that unnamed disciple and ask that Jesus teach us to pray as well.

Jesus began with the words, *"This is how you should pray..."* (NLT). Notice that Jesus did *not* say, *"This is **what** you should pray..."* Instead, He said, *"This is **how** you should pray..."* There is a big difference between the two. The one would be a prescribed prayer that must be followed. The other gives us a "model" that allows us the freedom of our own words.

The prayer consists of six petitions to God. The first three have to do with God and His glory. The other three have to do with our needs and necessities. It is a prayer that brings us into God's presence and also brings God into our everyday lives.

Speaking to God (6:9–10)

"Our Father in heaven"

Jesus' use of "our Father" reveals a dramatic new relationship between God and human beings. Those in the audience who heard Jesus would have been surprised. The Jews did not use this expression to address God. They would have probably begun with something like "Lord God of our fathers" or "God of Abraham." They would have considered "our Father" too personal. As disciples of Jesus, however, we have a new personal relationship with God.

Throughout the Gospels, Jesus often refers to God as "Father" or "my Father," showing the close personal relationship that He has with God. The followers of Jesus also share in a more personal relationship with God such as we see in the beginning of this prayer.

Jesus would have been speaking in Aramaic and would have probably used the expression *Abba*, which was an intimate name for a human father. It is a word used by little children for their father that implies the close personal relationship of parent to child. Some people may have carried Jesus' use of the word *abba* too far, suggesting that we call God "Daddy." We do know, however, that the early church adopted the use of the word *abba*, and Paul used the word in referring to God on two occasions (Romans 8:15; Galatians 4:6).

The words *in heaven* remind us to whom we are praying. This is no local deity, but rather the all-powerful, all-knowing Creator and sustainer of the universe.

"Hallowed be your name"

Hallowed is an older word that is not often used today. The word comes from the same root word as *holy* and means "to make holy" or "to sanctify." It is an expression that seeks to give honor, respect, and reverence to God's name.

Some versions translate the verse in a manner to show the meaning of the word. Examples include *"may your name be honored"* (NLT) and *"help us to honor your name"* (CEV).

In our contemporary culture in which God's name is so often misused and abused, how appropriate it is that the followers of Jesus should pray that God's name be honored.

"Your kingdom come"

Some people have equated the word *kingdom* entirely with the church and have said that it is inappropriate to pray this way today because the church is now in existence. To do so is to limit the meaning of the word *kingdom*. God's kingdom is the realm of His rule or reign and is used in the past, present, and future tenses in the Bible.

Both John the Baptist (Matthew 3:2) and Jesus (Matthew 4:17) had preached that the kingdom was near, and now Christians are a part of that kingdom as the church (Colossians 1:13). The church is God's kingdom here in the present, but God also reigns in heaven, so there is still a future aspect of God's kingdom yet to come for those who are faithful.

"Your will be done"

It may not be always easy for us to pray for God's will to be done. This is because sometimes we want our will to be done rather than God's will to be done. We must remember that God knows and sees everything and that He is always at work for the good of those who love Him (Romans 8:28).

How many times have we prayed for something, only to later see that it was not for the best? Also, we need to remember that Jesus prayed these same words in the Garden of Gethsemane as He faced the cross. That should be example enough for us in putting God's will first in our lives and prayers.

Making requests of God (6:11–13)

"Give us our daily bread"

Food, shelter, clothing — these are all basic things of life, and they all come from God. Even our ability to work to earn money for these things comes from God. We must be certain, however, that we are praying for what we need, not what we want. There can be a big difference.

Jesus called it "daily bread." Workers in the first century were paid by the day, and missing a day's work could be serious for a family living from hand to mouth.

Our work situation may be different, but God still gives us our necessities each day.

"Forgive us our debts"

Debts here mean sins or transgressions. We have much from which to be forgiven, and we need to remember this regularly in prayer. We also need to remember that our forgiveness is conditional. Jesus said, *"Forgive us our debts, as we also have forgiven our debtors."* Jesus taught more about this principle of forgiving others in the Parable of the Unforgiving Debtor (Luke 7:36–50). Here in Matthew 6, Jesus also teaches more about the conditional nature of forgiveness in verses 14–15.

"Lead us not into temptation"

God does not entice us to sin. We know this from the example of Jesus' own temptation and also from James's description of temptation and sin (James 1:13–15). The word can also mean a trial or testing. One writer suggests that Jesus was saying, *"Do not let us fall into a trial so difficult that we will fail."*[1] We know that we will have temptations. We are asking God to not allow us to be tempted beyond what we can withstand.

"Deliver us from the evil one"

We live in a lost and fallen world. Both Satan and evil are real. Paul wrote to the Christians in Ephesus of the *"powers of the dark world"* (Ephesians 6:12) and of the *"dominion of darkness"* from which believers must be rescued (Colossians 1:13). Peter described the devil as a lion seeking out victims (1 Peter 5:8).

---

1.   Robert Mounce, *Matthew, New International Biblical Commentary,* (Peabody, MA: Hendrickson, 1991), 57.

In this model prayer, Jesus encouraged His followers to pray that God may deliver them from Satan and his power. It is an aspect of prayer that we often neglect.

More on forgiveness (6:14–16)

The prayer itself ends in verse 13. In verses 14–15, Jesus continued the thought found in verse 12 about forgiving others. In these last verses, we see that forgiveness is conditional on our forgiving others. This is not always an easy thing to do. It is much easier to hold a grudge or want to get back at the other person rather than to forgive the person. Once again, it is apparent that the followers of Jesus are to be different from the surrounding culture and be willing to forgive those who hurt them.

PEAK REFLECTIONS

1. How did Jesus' addressing God as "Our Father" differ from typical prayers of that time? What does this tell us about our relationship with God?
2. What does the word *hallowed* mean? How can we "hallow" God's name?
3. What is the kingdom of God? In what different ways is the word used in the Bible?
4. "Daily bread" seems to imply more than just food. What are some other "daily" needs that God supplies?
5. What do verses 14–15 tell us about forgiveness? What is our responsibility in forgiveness?

Whatever we *value* most... will determine our *loyalty*, either to **God** or to our **possessions**.

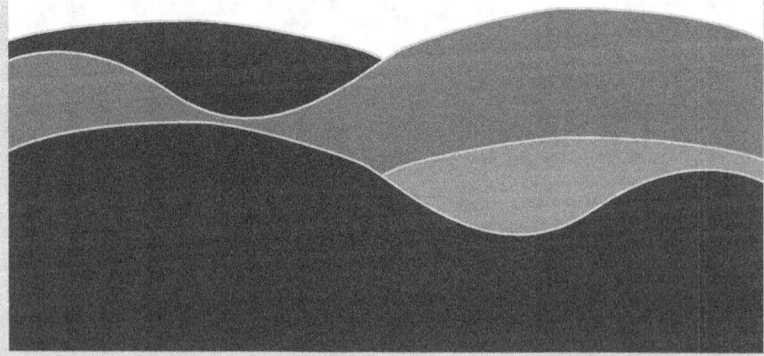

Eight

View from the Top

Treasures in Heaven
Matthew 6:19–24

As children, we soon learn the value of money. From a child's toy truck to an adult's luxury car or designer clothing, we begin to realize the seeming value of material things. It should not surprise us, then, that much of Jesus' teaching was concerned with money and possessions and how they should be properly used. Today, we have financial advisors to tell us what to do with our finances, but Jesus' plan is much simpler and has an eternal reward.

The Parable of the Rich Fool, Parable of the Rich Man and Lazarus, the story of the Rich Young Ruler, and even the Parable of the Sheep and Goats are all examples of Jesus' teaching on how to properly and responsibly use possessions. Here, in the Sermon on the Mount, Jesus brought what He taught elsewhere into a few simple illustrations that are easily understood, but perhaps difficult to follow.

"Do not store up for yourselves treasures on earth" (6:19–21)

The first illustration that Jesus used was a comparison between earthly treasures and treasures in heaven. There were various kinds of "treasures" in the ancient world. The gifts brought to baby Jesus by the magi are examples (Matthew 2:11). Silver, gold, or precious stones were often hidden or buried for safety. Jesus' Parable of the Hidden Treasure (Matthew 13:44) is an example of this practice. Wealth was sometimes measured as oil or grain that was stored away and sold. All of these would have been valued possessions.

Jesus did not say that it was wrong to have possessions. The Bible nowhere forbids a person from having private property. The children of Israel were given the Promised Land as a possession. Some of the great characters of the Bible, such as Abraham and Job, were wealthy. Christians are free to put aside something for the future, including things like savings accounts, life insurance, and retirement annuities. To do otherwise would not be responsible and could cause us to become a burden on others or place a hardship on our family.

What Jesus did forbid His followers from doing is the selfish accumulation of possessions. Selfishness, greed, and covetousness — these are the things that Jesus' disciples are to avoid.

Much of Jesus' teaching dealt with the responsibility of using our possessions to help others in need. The Parable of Rich Man and Lazarus (Luke 16:19–31) is one story that Jesus used to illustrate this. In the story, there are two characters, a rich man and a beggar named Lazarus. The rich man lived in luxury and would be comparable to the ultra-rich of today. Every day as he went in and out of his house, he passed Lazarus, lying at his gate begging for something to sustain himself, but the rich man ignored him. William Barclay calls him *"the man who never noticed."*[1] At the end of the story, Lazarus died and was taken by angels to an eternal reward. The rich man also died, but he was sent to be punished.

Lazarus was not good or righteous just because he was poor, and the rich man was not bad just because he was rich. The rich man was condemned because he failed to share with others. The rich man had accumulated wealth, but it was only "treasure on earth," and he had failed to store away any "treasure in heaven."

Although there is no mention of treasures, Jesus' Parable of the Sheep and Goats (Matthew 25:31–46) does have a similar meaning. Those in the parable who were blessed had helped others, while those who were condemned had failed to use their earthly treasures to help others.

As appealing to us as money or material things may be, Jesus reminds us that "earthly treasures" are only temporary. Such "treasures" will not last forever and

---

1. William Barclay, *The Gospel of Luke*, 252.

can easily be destroyed or stolen. He mentions that moths could eat and destroy clothing, metal objects could rust or corrode, and thieves could break into a house and steal valuables. Instead of "earthly treasures," that can be stolen or destroyed, Jesus tells His disciples to store up "treasures in heaven." These are nothing at all like earthly treasures. As John Stott described them in *The Cross for Christ*: *"to 'lay up treasure in heaven' is to do anything on earth whose effects last for eternity."*[2]

Verse 21 is really the key to understanding Jesus' words: *"For where your treasure is, there your heart will be also."* "Heart" is here used figuratively as the seat of emotions and values. Whatever we value most, where we put our treasure, will determine our loyalty, either to God or to our possessions. Which is more important: an "earthly treasure" that can be stolen or destroyed, or a "heavenly treasure" that will last forever? This question calls each of us to examine our priorities and to consider where our true devotion lies. It challenges us to invest in what has eternal value rather than what is temporary.

The eye and the body (6:22–23)

At first glance, verses 22–23 may seem to be out of place, but they are actually a part of Jesus' lesson on possessions. In Jesus' day, the "eye" was thought to be a window into the body. The "eye" was also used figuratively much like we use the word *heart* today. Jesus was not speaking of the physical "eye," but rather of our inner being.

Jesus contrasted a "good" or "healthy" eye with a "bad" or "unhealthy" eye. In other words, Jesus was

---

2.   John R. W. Scott, *The Message of the Sermon on the Mount*, 156.

describing the right way and the wrong way of looking at things. If our vision is clear, then our hearts will be right, and we will have the right priorities. If our vision is clouded by what John Stott calls *"the gods of material- ism,"* then our values and priorities will be wrong.

At that time, the "good" and "bad" eye was also used figuratively in another way. The "good" or "healthy" eye was used to signify devotion and loyalty to God as well as generosity toward others. The "bad" or "unhealthy" eye was used in the opposite way to suggest a lack of obedience toward God or a jealous and stingy attitude. This way of looking at these metaphors fits in even better with the overall subject of Jesus' teaching on how to use possessions in this passage.

"No one can serve two masters" (6:24)

Jesus closed this part of His teaching by saying, "No one can serve two masters." The word *serve* comes from the same root word as *slave*, which gives a special emphasis to His words. Jesus is referring to a master/ slave relationship, one in which the master is in total control.

The words *love* and *hate* describe a pattern of living or a way of life rather than simply emotions. Jesus was saying that a person must totally serve one master or the other. You cannot serve both, but must make a choice between the two. Jesus actually personified wealth or possessions as a rival god, which He called *Mamon*, an Aramaic word for "money" or "wealth." The effective- ness of this illustration is somewhat lost in the versions that translate the word as "money."

As far as Jesus is concerned, it is one or the other, not both. A writer named Matthew Green explained it this way: *"God has to come first, and money a poor second... you cannot be devoted to God if you are devoted to money and the things money will buy."*[3]

We can also see an example of someone who served the god of possessions in the Parable of the Rich Fool (Luke 12:13–21). He had been richly blessed by God, but instead of sharing this with others, he planned to build bigger barns to store his wealth for himself.

We see from the story that God had other plans. In verse 20 we read, *"But God said to him, 'You fool! This very night your life will be demanded from you. Then who will get what you have prepared for yourself?'"* Then in the next verse Jesus added, *"This is how it will be with anyone who stores up things for himself but is not rich toward God."*

The saying, "The one who dies with the most toys wins," may be the way that many people look at possessions, but it is totally contrary to Jesus' teachings. Jesus did not say that everyone who follows Him must give away all of their possessions. That would not be practical.

What Jesus did say was that His followers should put their treasure in the right place. God has given us everything that we have, but He expects us to use it properly, such as to care for ourselves and our family, to help others in need, and to support the work of God's kingdom both here and around the world. By using our possessions in the way that God wants, we can store up for ourselves treasures in heaven.

---

3.   Michael Green, *The Message of Matthew* (Downers Grove, IL: InterVarsity Press, 2000), 102, 103.

PEAK REFLECTIONS

1. Why did Jesus spend so much time teaching about possessions?
2. What is the difference between an earthly treasure and a treasure in heaven?
3. What are some ways to deposit treasures in heaven?
4. How do verses 22–23 connect with the rest of this passage?
5. How would you explain verse 24? How does this verse capture the meaning of the rest of Jesus' teachings on properly using our possessions?

Christians should be known for **faith** and **trust** in *God*.

Nine

A Faith That Moves Mountains

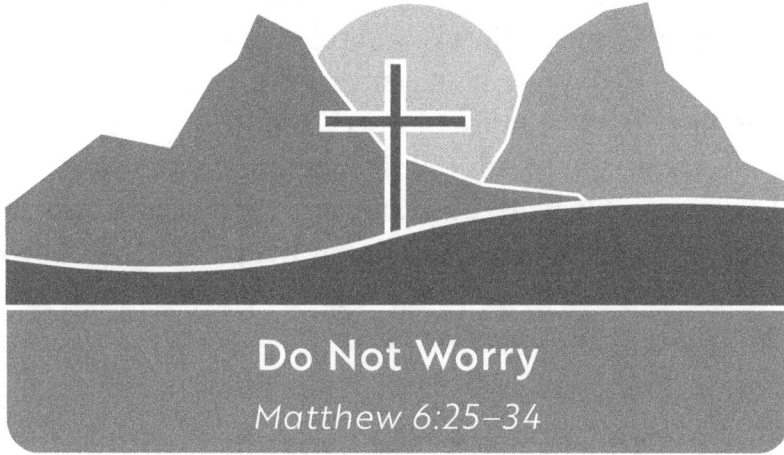

Do Not Worry
Matthew 6:25–34

Jesus' words, "Do not worry…," speak to all of us because we all have our own worries. It would be easy to dismiss His words by saying, "Oh, that was a simpler time. I have a lot more to worry about today." That is true to some extent, but just think for a moment what it must have been like to have lived in the first century. Infant mortality was high, and deaths from childhood diseases were common. The average life expectancy was about 35–40 years of age. There were no hospitals and what medical care was available was limited. Antibiotics, immunization, and even common pain relievers, such as aspirin, were unknown. There was no Social Security, medical insurance, Medicare, or retirement. Most of those who heard Jesus worked hard just to provide the minimum clothing, food, and shelter for themselves and their families. In addition to those conditions, Jesus' original hearers lived in a land that had been conquered many times by invading armies and was at the time subject to a foreign nation. If anything, life in Jesus' day was much more difficult than today, and people had much more to worry about.

So how could Jesus tell His audience not to worry or be anxious? It is because He gave them a new way of looking at life and a new way of living. This had been His message all through the Sermon on the Mount, and we will see it again as we begin this lesson.

God will supply the basics (6:25–30)

One of the first things that you will notice in reading this passage is that the word *worry* or *anxious* is used several times in these verses (vv. 25, 27, 28, 31, 34). The original word means literally "to be divided or distracted." It can mean "to be anxious," "to worry," "to be troubled with care," or "to be concerned." Elsewhere in the New Testament, we find the word in Philippians 2:20 translated in different versions as "concern," "interest, or "care" and in Philippians 4:6 as "anxious" or "worry." In 1 Peter 5:7 the same word is translated as "worries," "care," or "anxieties," depending on the version. Perhaps one of the best ways to understand the meaning of the word is found in Jesus' description of Martha, the multitasking, overly distracted, stressed-out sister of Mary and Lazarus (Luke 10:41).

The words *worry* or *anxious* as used in the New Testament should not be confused with the technical term *anxiety*. This is used to describe an emotional problem that can be serious and may require counseling or even medical treatment. This is not what Jesus was talking about. He was referring to the concern or worry that all of us experience at times.

Jesus was not saying that His followers should not make plans for the future or not have legitimate concerns about our needs or the needs of others. Some worry or concern is sometimes necessary. A sick child or driving on a dark, unfamiliar road are examples of situations needing extra concern or care. Jesus was talking more about worry that consumes and controls a person's life.

William Barclay suggests this definition for the original Greek word found in Matthew: *"to worry anxiously."*[1] That seems to capture the meaning of Jesus' thoughts well. Barclay also gives some examples of the use of the same word from everyday writings from around the first century, such as a wife worried or concerned about her husband's safe return and a mother writing of her concern for her son's welfare. These examples are similar to the worry or care that we all have in our lives. It is when this worry takes over, preventing a person from living a normal everyday life, that things go wrong.

Jesus was speaking to people who struggled daily for the basic necessities of life: food, clothing, and shelter. His comments were personal and meaningful for His audience. We live in a different world, but Jesus' words still have meaning. This is because what Jesus was really

1.   William Barclay, *The Gospel of Matthew Volume 1*, 255.

doing was to give His followers priorities. Some things are more important in life than others. This does not mean that we don't need food or that we should run around without clothes!

Jesus next used some analogies from nature to make His point. The first of these was the birds that do not plant, harvest crops, or store up food, yet God feeds them (v. 26). That is not to say that birds are lazy. Like all other animals in the natural world, birds spend much time and energy in feeding, building nests, and other activities. The point is that God, in His creation, has provided for them. Jesus' second example from nature was the flowers that grow naturally in the wild. Anyone who has taken the time to look at the structure, color, and beauty of flowers can understand Jesus' thoughts here. As Jesus explained, however, flowers are more beautiful than all the riches of Solomon could provide, yet they do not spin, weave cloth, or make clothing.

Jesus encouraged His followers to rely on God to care for them as He cares for the birds and plants. This is a type of argument known as from "lesser to greater." If God takes care of birds and flowers, won't He also take care of you?

Any number of books, programs, seminars, and other self-help resources are available today to aid in eliminating, or at least reducing, worry. Unfortunately, many of them don't work because they fail to get to the root of the problem. You can't just stop worrying. You have to replace it with something else. As we see in this lesson, Jesus' plan is to replace worry with putting God first, living right, and trusting in God's promise to care for us.

Worrying will not help (6:31–32)

Worrying achieves nothing and comes from a lack of faith. As William Barclay observed, *"Worry is essentially distrust in God."*[2] Robert Mounce in his commentary was even more pointed and described worry as *"practical atheism and an affront to God."*[3]

Worry cannot add a single hour to a person's life (v. 27) or make them any taller as in some versions. In fact, constant worry will probably shorten a person's life in the end.

In verse 32 Jesus said, *"The pagans run after these things."* In context, He was referring to food and clothing (v. 31), but we could add our own list of things that many "run after." The word *pagans* here refers to non-Jewish people or Gentiles. They were unbelievers, those who lived without God. The pagans believed in unpredictable gods/goddesses and constantly sought to appease them so that they would give them good things. They never knew how their god/goddess would respond, so they lived in a constant state of fear and anxiety. We could compare these people to those today who do not follow God and put all their energy into striving for the things of this world. Jesus called people like this literally "little-faiths." Jesus said not to be like them. Put your faith in God instead.

Having the right priorities will reduce our worries (6:33–34)

Verse 33 may be the most important thought in all of the Sermon on the Mount. Seeking the kingdom of God first

---

2.   William Barclay, *The Gospel of Matthew Volume 1*, 258.
3.   Robert Mounce, *Matthew*, New International Biblical Commentary (Peabody, MA: Hendrickson, 1991), 61.

in our lives is the most important thing that anyone can do. When a person puts God first, Jesus said, *"all these other things will be given to you as well."*

Seeking God's kingdom first places the emphasis on spiritual things rather than material things. It is to put first things first and not be continually distracted. This should be the number one priority in the lives of Jesus' followers. When you put God first, worrying will decrease and everything else will fall into place.

A simple way to summarize verse 34 is to just live one day at a time. This is often easier said than done. Jesus was saying to take one day as it comes and not to worry about things that may never happen. Every day has enough troubles for itself; why worry about tomorrow's problems as well?

This serves as a reminder that God did not promise a trouble-free life for His people. Today has its problems and so will tomorrow. The wise man Job put it this way: *"Man born of woman is of few days and full of trouble"* (Job 14:1). Worrying about what might happen will not help. Only trusting in God and His care can get us through the troubles ahead.

Some popular preachers of today may tell you that becoming a Christian will solve all your problems. Jesus was much more realistic: "Each day has enough trouble of its own." This does not mean that Jesus was a pessimist. His message was simple: God will give you what you need and try not to worry about the rest.

We all have things in life that we worry about. If, however, we are going to keep worry from controlling our lives, then we will need to take Jesus' advice and put God first and allow Him to take care of the big things that we cannot take care of ourselves.

As we have noticed more than once before, the followers of Jesus are to be different. Unlike those who go through life rushing around, worrying, and seeking after the things of this world, Christians should be known for faith and trust in God. It is only by allowing God to be first and putting worry aside that we can live the life that He wants us to live.

PEAK REFLECTIONS

1. When does everyday care or concern become controlling worry?
2. What examples of worry did Jesus give? What sort of things do we worry about today?
3. What are some ways that we can avoid excessive worry in our lives?
4. What does it mean to seek God's kingdom first in our lives? What has to be done first before a person can do this?
5. What was Jesus' final thought in verse 34? Why is it often so hard to do this?

As *followers* of Jesus, we need to be able to determine **right** from wrong and **good** from evil.

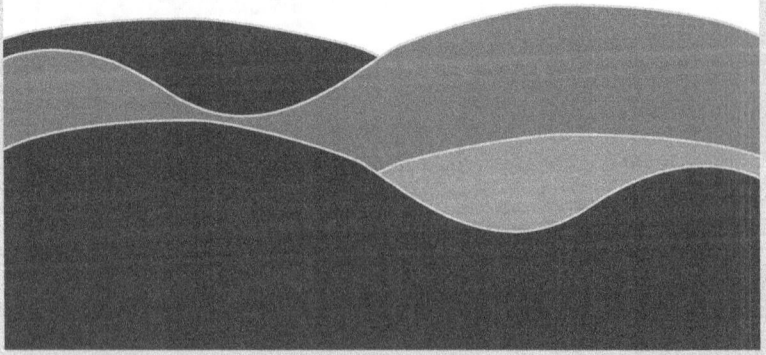

Ten

Pass On

Do Not Judge
Matthew 7:1–5

Matthew 6 ends with Jesus teaching that His followers are to give first priority to seeking righteousness and the kingdom of God (Matthew 6:33). Once a person is right with God, then relationships with other people will be affected as well. The first of these that Jesus mentioned involves judging others. Anyone who has experienced harsh, judgmental criticism from another person will appreciate Jesus' words.

Do not set yourself up as a judge of others (7:1–2)

Jesus began this part of the Sermon on the Mount by saying, *"Do not judge, or you too will be judged"* (NIV). Some form of the word *judge* is used four times in these two verses. The original word means "to judge" or "to pass judgment." It can also mean "to condemn," and that is the sense that it is used here.

The same word is found in Luke 6:37 in a similar statement by Jesus. It is also used in James 2:1-4 to describe the prejudicial treatment of one person over another. Here in Matthew 7, it is used to describe judging in a fault-finding, condemning attitude while overlooking our own faults and amplifying the faults of others.

Some writers have compared Jesus' teaching here with what is called the Parable of the Unmerciful Servant or Parable of the Unforgiving Debtor (Matthew 18:21–35). In this parable, one man was forgiven a tremendously large debt, but he was unwilling to forgive another man who owed him a small amount. In the end, he was punished for his unwillingness to forgive others as he had been forgiven himself.

We see in the parable that being forgiven is dependent on being willing to forgive others. The same is true of judging other people. With God, judging goes both ways. The way in which we judge others will determine how we will be judged.

The speck and the beam (7:3–5)

Jesus was a storyteller, and He used a vivid, even humorous, illustration to explain the meaning of His statement. It was an illustration, as one writer described it, that came from the carpenter's shop. The "speck" or "speck of sawdust" was a small foreign body in the eye of another person. The "beam," "plank," or "log" was a big chunk of wood in your own eye. The word literally referred to a beam used to support the roof of a building. This was obviously a hyperbole. It was an exaggerated figure of speech that Jesus used for emphasis. Jesus used hyperboles on other occasions, such as the camel going through the eye of a needle (Matthew 19:24) and the straining of a gnat and swallowing of a camel (Matthew 23:24). We can imagine the smiles, even laughter, that resulted from this illustration. Such exaggerations helped people to remember the story and the meaning that Jesus gave to it.

Some have called this illustration ludicrous, but Jesus made His point. Jesus used this hyperbole to teach a simple lesson: Don't be looking for the faults of others when you have major problems of your own. He called those who did this hypocrites or "play actors." Jesus had used this term earlier to describe those who tried to make themselves look good to others. Here He used *hypocrites* to describe those who set themselves up as judges.

The speck/beam illustration reminds us that we ourselves are fallible and fallen human beings. Just like our brother with the speck of dust in his eye, we are also sinners. Because we are sinners, we are not in a good position to stand in judgment of others. It is hypocritical to condemn others for their minor faults when we have major problems of our own. Before we can correct others, we need to correct our own faults.

Jesus was not saying that His followers must ignore the faults of others.

As followers of Jesus, we need to be able to determine right from wrong and good from evil. Jesus spoke in verses 15– 20 of this same chapter about recognizing false prophets by their actions. At times, Jesus clearly pointed out the wrongs of others, such as the Pharisees and other religious leaders.

What Jesus did forbid was harsh, critical, and judgmental fault-finding that ignores our own shortcomings and emphasizes the failures of others. There is a human tendency to minimize our own faults and exaggerate the faults of others.

Jesus illustrated this in the Parable of the Pharisee and the Tax Collector in Luke 18:9–14. In this parable, all that the Pharisee could do was to magnify his own goodness and compare this with the limitations of others. The tax collector was quite the opposite. All that he could do was to realize his own sinfulness and beg for God's mercy.

Jesus was especially critical of the Pharisee for having this self-righteous and critical attitude. It is interesting to note that in our own language the word *pharisee* is used to refer to a self-righteous and judgmental person.

In verse 2 Jesus expanded the "do not judge" statement by adding that we will be judged in the same way that we judge others. That puts things in a whole different light. Would I want to be judged myself by a harsh, critical standard? Obviously, I would not want to be judged in that manner. I would rather be judged fairly and impartially, and Jesus is saying that is how we should judge others.

It is possible, however, to carry the idea of not being a judge too far. Today, many people try to use Jesus' teaching concerning judging others to justify their own behavior or to promote "tolerance" that will accept almost any type of behavior. Was this Jesus' intention? Was He merely teaching that people should be "tolerant," in the sense in which the word is used today?

When we look at the Gospels, we see that Jesus was accepting of others. In fact, He was often criticized for associating with tax collectors and those that the religious leaders called "sinners."

There is, however, a difference between accepting others and being "tolerant." It is possible to accept a person as a fellow human being and made in God's image, yet not approve of how that person is living his or her life. Yes, Jesus accepted people, but He did not leave them where they were. He always encouraged them to move on, to leave their sins behind, and to draw closer to God.

An excellent example of this was Jesus' encounter with the woman who was caught in adultery (John 7:53-8:11). Those present were ready to stone the woman, but Jesus diverted their attention with His statement, *"Let any one of you who is without sin be the first to throw a stone at her"* (NIV). The crowd dispersed until only Jesus and the woman were left. Looking at her, Jesus said, *"Woman, where are they? Has no one condemned you?"* And then He said, *"Then neither do I condemn you. Go now and leave your life of sin."*

Jesus did not condemn the woman, but that does not mean that He did not judge her behavior to be immoral and wrong. As William Barclay has observed, Jesus *"did not say: 'It is all right; don't worry; just go on as you are doing.' He said: 'It's all wrong... change your life from top to bottom; go and sin no more.'"*[1] Jesus freely accepted this woman, but

---

1. William Barclay, *The Gospel of John Volume 2* (Philadelphia: Westminster Press, 1975), 8.

rather than being "tolerant" of her lifestyle, He challenged her to change for the better.

Dogs and pigs (7:6)

At first, verse 6 may seem to have nothing to do with Jesus' teaching on judging others in the previous verses. Looking at it more closely, we will see that Jesus was still talking about judging, but it is a different type of judging.

In verse 6 Jesus was explaining how His disciples must learn to discriminate in sharing the Good News with others.

Some people are open and willing to learn, but others will reject God and His kingdom. Jesus used these graphic illustrations of the dogs and pigs to describe individuals like this.

It involves judging a person's character but is not the same type of judging that Jesus condemned in verses 1–5. It is a warning not to share spiritual truths with those who are unable or unwilling to accept them. Or in simpler terms, don't waste your time trying to teach someone who is not willing to listen.

To make that decision, the disciple will have to judge the motives and attitude of another person, using the guidelines that Jesus has given in verses 1–5.

Looking at Jesus' teaching, we see a lot of practical wisdom as well as several things that we must remember before deciding to judge another person. First of all, we may not know the whole story. There may be circumstances that we know nothing about, and there may also be more than one side to the story.

Secondly, it is difficult to be impartial. We all have our own prejudices and emotions that can affect our thinking. Additionally, it is so easy to see another person's problems and exaggerate the faults of others while minimizing our own.

Thirdly, there is no one good enough to be a judge of others. Only God is completely holy and good enough to do that.

Finally, from my own experience I would add — if we take care of our own problems, then we will not have much time left to worry about the problems of others.

PEAK REFLECTIONS

1. Why is it so much easier to see the faults of others and ignore our own?

2. What did Jesus say would happen to us if we judge others in a harsh, critical manner? How does that change the situation?

3. How do parables like the Pharisee and the Tax Collector and the Unforgiving Servant mentioned in this lesson add to our understanding of Jesus' teaching on judging others?

4. How did Jesus' hyperbole of the speck and beam make His teaching more interesting and easier to remember?

5. As Christians, we must be able to recognize right from wrong behavior. How is this different from setting ourselves up as judges? What should be the standard for making such decisions?

Prayer is
an **ongoing**
relationship
rather than
a **casual**
acquaintance.

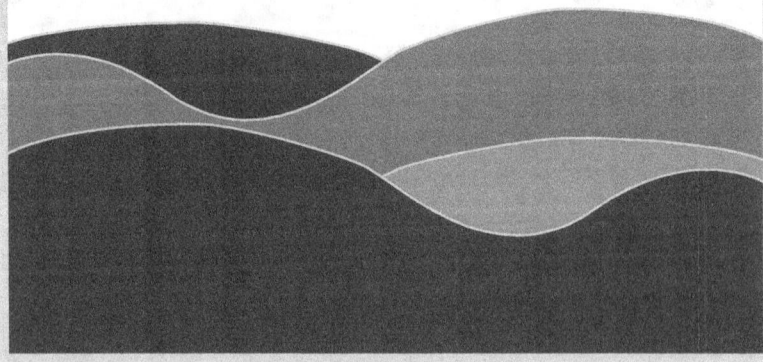

Eleven

Within His Reach

Ask, Seek, Knock
Matthew 7:7–11

Some of the most meaningful and sincere prayers are spoken by small children and new Christians. Perhaps it is because they have not yet realized the full implications of prayer. After all, it isn't easy to talk with Someone that you cannot see or hear, especially if that Someone is an all-powerful, all-knowing God who created and sustains the universe. Perhaps that is why Jesus spent so much time teaching about prayer in simple language that most anyone could understand.

In our previous lessons, we have looked at some of Jesus' teaching on prayer found in the Sermon on the Mount. In Matthew 6:5–8, Jesus spoke about having the proper attitude in prayer. In Matthew 6:9–13, Jesus gave His followers a "model prayer." Here in Matthew 7, Jesus approaches prayer in a different way.

Some people have looked at Jesus' statement here in Matthew 7 as a sort of "Christmas list." Some popular evangelists may tell you that all we need to do is ask for something, and God will give it. Is that what Jesus was saying, or was He telling His followers something else about prayer? Anyone who has had any "life experience" will realize that there is much more to prayer than simply asking for whatever you want.

Ask, seek, and knock (7:7–8)

Once again, Jesus returned to the subject of prayer. This time He is teaching about the need to pray regularly and continuously as well a little about the nature of God and how He answers prayers.

Jesus used repetition to emphasize His meaning. Jesus did not just say pray; He said to ask, to seek, and to knock. There is an emphasis on persistence in the words themselves. We do not immediately see this in English, but in the original language, these are continuous action verbs. A few translations indicate this continuous action. One version, for example, translated this verse as: *"So, I tell you, continue asking, and it will be given to you. Keep on searching, and you will find. Be knocking, and the door will open for you"* (IEB). Another version is even a little more emphatic: *"Keep on asking, and you will receive what you ask for. Keep on seeking, and you will find. Keep on knocking, and the door will be opened to you"* (NLT).

The words themselves also convey slightly different meanings. *Ask* implies praying with humility and a consciousness of our needs. We ask God for specific blessings, or we ask God for forgiveness of sins, for example. *Seek* suggests praying actively and trying to determine God's will in our lives. *Knock* has the idea of persistence in prayer and gives the impression of a person knocking repeatedly on a door, seeking admission.

In verse 8, Jesus assures us that asking, seeking, and knocking are not merely mental exercises. God will hear and answer these prayers in His own time and in His own way.

Human gifts and God's gifts (7:9–11)

Jesus also used the example of human parents to illustrate His meaning.

In a way similar to the parables, Jesus used this earthly story as an illustration.

He used a comparison between the parents' desire to give gifts to children and God's generosity toward those who ask, seek, and knock. His point is this: If human parents give good gifts to children, won't God give much more to those who ask?

It is interesting to note that the word *give* is used five times in these verses. It is actually the key to understanding these verses. In Jesus' example, human fathers will give gifts to their children, but God is so much greater. God's gifts are called "good gifts" (v. 11). What God gives may not be exactly what was requested, but it will be a "good gift." It will be the best answer to the prayer. Only God has the divine perspective to respond to each request in the best way.

Is there more to prayer than this? Yes. Prayer is a complex subject, and we must consider other teachings on prayer as well. Three of Jesus' parables deal directly with prayer. One of them, the Parable of the Pharisee and the Tax Collector (Luke 18:9–14), we discussed in a previous lesson. This parable shows that a person must pray with humility and awareness of personal weaknesses and faults. The other two, the Parable of the Persistent Widow (Luke 18:1–8) and the Parable of the Friend at Midnight (Luke 11:5-8) are more related to what Jesus was teaching here in the Sermon on the Mount.

The details are different in these two parables, but the meaning is much the same. In one, a widow persists in approaching a judge to aid her in a legal matter. In the other, a man wakes up his neighbor at night asking for bread to feed a guest. Both the judge and the neighbor were initially resistant, but eventually gave into the requests.

Any interpretation of these parables that suggests that God is reluctant to grant our requests and must be worn down is incorrect. These are parables that teach us to not give up on prayer, but rather to make prayer a continuous part of our relationship with God (Luke 18:1).

Other things to consider about prayer

Prayer is an ongoing relationship rather than a casual acquaintance. Many people will tell you that they pray, but they have few, if any, religious convictions and no real relationship with God. They go along on their own until something bad happens to them, and then they run to God and want Him to take care of it. God does not want to be just a troubleshooter; He wants to be an integral part of your life, and prayer is necessary for that connection.

Prayer requires faith. Jesus said, *"Therefore I tell you, whatever you ask for in prayer, believe that you have received it, and it will be yours"* (Mark 11:24). That is a powerful thought. Again, it goes back to this idea of a trusting, faithful relationship with God.

Prayer must also be based on God's will, not our own will. John wrote, *"This is the confidence we have in approaching God: that if we ask anything according to his will, he hears us"* (1 John 5:14). Sometimes it is not easy to know God's will. Sometimes it is not easy to give up our own will. Jesus is our example in this. Everything He did, even going to the cross, was within God's will.

We should pray for what we need and not what we want. This isn't always easy. Sometimes we want more that we need but remember Jesus' model prayer. He included only the basics.

How to pray is something that we must learn. Remember from a previous lesson, that the disciples went to Jesus and asked Him, *"Lord, teach us to pray"* (Luke 11:1). That should be our attitude and desire as well.

There is also the big question: How does God answer prayers? If you think about it, God answers prayers in one of three ways: yes, no, or wait a while. If God answers "yes," then we will generally be happy and pleased with the result. If God answers "no," then we will likely be disappointed, at least initially. It is likely, however, that, in time, we will come to see that God's refusal was the best answer. After all, God knows a lot more than we do and can look into the future and see the outcome of our prayers.

It is the "wait a while" answer that is, at times, most difficult to comprehend. How do you tell a "no" from a "wait a while"? It isn't always easy. It takes time and patience to understand the difference. We are certainly not alone in dealing with the "wait a while" answers. The Bible has many examples of those who prayed and waited — many of them for long periods of time.

As we noticed previously, those who were with Jesus had a desire to improve in their prayer lives. I recall the story of a man who wanted to become a great "prayer warrior," so he got up at 5:00 in the morning to pray and read the Bible. His good intentions lasted a little while, but soon, his mind began to wander, and eventually, he fell asleep. Discouraged by his weakness and failure, he gave up his lofty goal and tried to just do his best when he prayed to God.

I don't know about you, but I can see myself in that story. I look at all the books on prayer online and in the Christian bookstores and think, *Wow! Those folks must be experts on prayer.* I listen to someone pray and think how inadequate my prayers must be. In reality, however, prayer is personal and as individual as each of us, and imitating someone else's prayers doesn't necessarily make one's own prayers any better.

The key to learning to pray is in Jesus' own words: keep asking, keep seeking, and keep knocking. In other words, keep in communication with God. That is the key to prayer.

PEAK REFLECTIONS

1. What does the fact that the words *ask*, *seek*, and *knock* are continuous action verbs in the original language tell us about Jesus' attitude toward prayer?

2. Some people may see Jesus' statement about asking, seeking, and knocking as some sort of wish list. Why is this not the case?

3. What are some requirements or prerequisites for effective prayer?

4. What are some additional insights on prayer that we can learn from the parables mentioned in this lesson?

5. What do we learn further about prayer from passages such as 1 Thessalonians 5:16–18 and James 5:13? How do these relate to Jesus' teaching on prayer here in the Sermon on the Mount?

If you **treat** *others* the way that *you* want to be **treated**, you cannot go wrong.

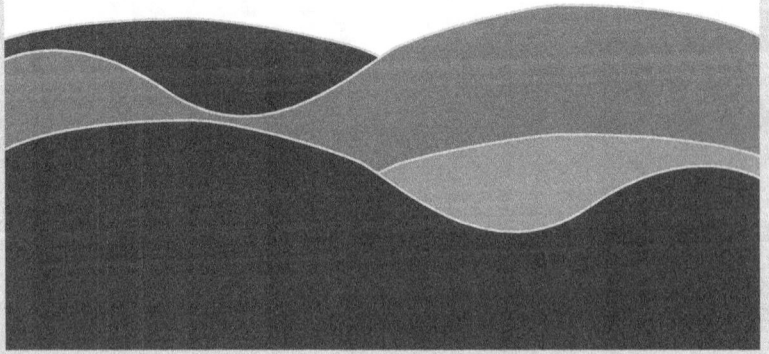

Twelve

Scaling New Heights

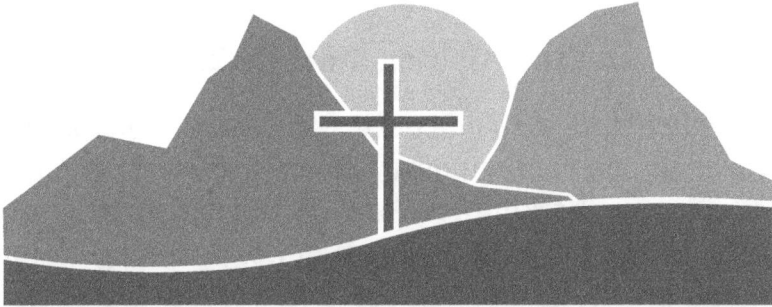

The "Golden Rule," Narrow and Wide Gates, Good and Bad Fruit, Two Kinds of Disciples
Matthew 7:12– 23

W e usually call, *"Treat others as you want them to treat you"* (CEV), the "Golden Rule." It has been described as the high point of the Sermon on the Mount. It is also one of the most well-known sayings of Jesus. Like most of the Sermon on the Mount, the "Golden Rule" was mainly intended for Jesus' followers, but could be practiced by anyone. It is a basic formula for human interactions. Instead of a long list of behaviors in various situations, Jesus gave this simple way to deal with other people in any situation.

Following verse 12, the remainder of the chapter contains four paragraphs, each contrasting two starkly different things. The last of these is in the form of a parable that we will look at in the next lesson.

The "Golden Rule" (7:12)

Showing kindness and courtesy to others is becoming rarer in our contemporary society, so much so, that simple acts of kindness are, at times, reported on the local or even the national news. Just imagine for a moment how different our world would be if most people practiced Jesus' command to treat others, as you would want to be treated yourself.

Actually, Jesus was not the only One to have made a statement like this. This saying, or at least one much like it, has been found in numerous writings. These include writings of Greek and Roman authors, as well as Jewish and other religious writings. In each of these other cases, however, the saying is in a negative form.

Confucius is reported to have said, *"What you do not want done to yourself, do not do to others."*[1] The Greek orator, Isocrates, said, *"Whatever angers you when you suffer it at the hands of others, do not do it to others."*[1] Rabbi Hillel stated it this way: *"What is hateful to you shall you not do to your neighbor..."*[2]

Jesus gave this saying in a positive form. The negative statements imply *not doing* anything: Don't do things to others that you do not like done to yourself.

---

1. These are both quoted in Robert Mounce, *Matthew*, 66.
2. Quoted in Jack P. Lewis, *The Gospel According to Matthew Part I 1:1–13:52* (Abilene: ACU Press, 1984), 113.

Jesus' statement means that we *must do* something: Treat others the way that we would like to be treated. Jesus calls for action — doing things for others that we would like to have done to us. This changes the whole meaning from "don't do this" to "do that." Jesus encouraged His followers to actively do good things for others, rather than just not treating them badly.

Jesus' words are associated with kindness and compassion and were exemplified in Jesus' life and how He treated others. We also see this in His teaching as well. The Parable of the Good Samaritan is one of the most prominent examples (Luke 10:25–37).

Jesus said that this statement *"sums up the Law and the Prophets."* In other words, all of God's teaching can be summed up in this one simple saying. That is powerful!

This is still true today. If you treat others the way that you want to be treated, you cannot go wrong. This was how Jesus lived, and this is how He wants His disciples to live as well.

The narrow and wide gates (7:13–14)

The Sermon on the Mount ends with a series of contrasting images. Those present in Jesus' original audience would have been familiar with this type of teaching. The Bible is filled with examples like this as well as major, contrasting themes like *light* and *darkness* and *good* and *bad*. The book of Proverbs in particular contains many such comparisons.

The first of these contrasts is the narrow and wide gates. It is likely that this illustration would have reminded Jesus' listeners of Psalm 1 that describes two ways of living.

It is a comparison of a faithful, obedient individual with those who live in rebellion toward God.

In these verses, Jesus pulled no punches, but rather was pointedly blunt. Being a follower or disciple of Jesus is not easy, and Jesus makes this abundantly clear.

William Barclay gave this passage the title: *"Life at the Crossroads."*[3] That is a good description of Jesus' teaching. A crossroads demands a decision, and that is what Jesus was talking about. At a crossroads, you must make a choice, because you can only go one way.

Jesus no doubt took His illustration from contemporary everyday life so that the people could understand Him. Ancient cities were typically surrounded by a wall for defense, and those walls were gates. Some were large enough for a wagon or cart to pass through, while others were so narrow that only a single person or perhaps a small donkey could pass through. Jesus gave this illustration spiritual significance.

He spoke of a small gate and narrow road and a wide gate and broad road. Some versions translate the word as "way" rather than "road." Either one is correct. Psalm 1:6 contrasts the *"way of the righteous"* and the *"way of the wicked."* Jesus called Himself *"the way"* in John 14:6. The church is also called *"the way"* in the book of Acts (Acts 9:2: 19:9, 23; 24:14,22). Obviously, these are referring to the narrow way.

The wide gate and broad road or way is the easy way, and most people take that road. This is the way of self-centeredness. No one tells you what to do on this road. It is up to you. You make the rules.

The broad way is the way of least resistance. If you follow the crowd, you will be on the wide road.

---

3.   William Barclay, *The Gospel of Matthew, Volume 1.*

Unfortunately, it only leads to destruction. It is the ultimate fate of the disobedient and rebellious.

In the same context, Jesus also spoke of the small gate and the narrow way. This road is narrow and hard to find, but it is the right way to go. It is the way of commitment and discipleship. The narrow way is not the easy way. It may, at times, be hard to follow, but it is the only way that leads to life. Not just physical life, but eternal life, the reward of the faithful followers of Jesus. In John 3:16, we read that those who believe in Jesus *"shall not perish but have eternal life."* This is the narrow way, the way to life eternal. In John 10:10, Jesus said that He had come to give a full or abundant life. It is the same life to which He referred here in the Sermon on the Mount.

The good and bad fruit (7:15–20)

Jesus began this section by talking about prophets. A prophet was someone who spoke for God. We tend to think of a prophet as a person who predicts the future. This is only a part of the role of the prophet. In Bible times, the prophets also communicated God's Word to others. In other words, prophets were also teachers. This was especially important in the early church. There was yet no New Testament, and the early disciples relied on the apostles and others who could teach them God's Word.

The problem was that not all prophets (or teachers) were true to God. Jesus called them *"false prophets."* Jesus said that they were like wolves in sheep's clothing. This is, of course, a metaphor, but it is graphic way of describing such individuals. They looked like one thing but were really another. They came, claiming to have a message from God, but actually it was not. Because they looked and talked like a prophet or teacher, people would believe them, even though their message was false.

Twice, Jesus said, *"by their fruit you shall know them"* (vv. 16, 20). This is obviously figurative language. "Fruit" is a metaphor describing their teaching. He used the simple illustration: Good fruit comes from good plants, but bad fruit comes from bad plants. This was just common sense. If you are out in the woods, you don't eat everything that looks good. Some of those red berries may be poisonous. You should only eat fruit that you know is good.

Jesus used this as an analogy. If a prophet's message doesn't seem to come from God, or if his lifestyle is wrong, then he must be a false prophet. The same is true today. If the "fruit" of an evangelist or teacher does not look good, then don't accept the teachings.

Two kinds of followers (7:21–23)

In this third comparison, Jesus used a sobering image of the judgment and end of time to illustrate His point. Jesus described the sad fate of false prophets. They claimed to be serving God, but in reality, they only served themselves. We have examples of this today in some of the popular ministers and televangelists who used their positions and popularity for their own personal gain.

Many people may claim to be followers of Jesus, but Jesus will not recognize those who have not done God's will. For this reason, we must diligently study to know God's will and then do it. Merely claiming to be a disciple is not enough.

From the Golden Rule to the judgment scene, these verses may at first seem to be disconnected. When we look at them more carefully, however, we see that they are connected by the central theme of the Sermon on the Mount: Jesus' disciples are to be different from the world and those around them.

PEAK REFLECTIONS

1. How is Jesus' positive statement of the Golden Rule different from other negative forms of similar statements?
2. Why is the Golden Rule applicable in almost any situation?
3. Why is the wide gate or broad way so appealing to many people?
4. How did Jesus say that we should recognize false or teachers?
5. What do verses 21–23 tell us about serving God?

Jesus demands
two things:
to *listen*
and *know*
His words
and then to
follow them.

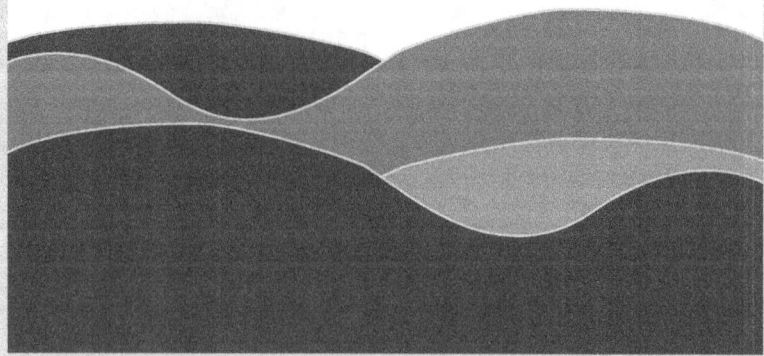

Thirteen

On the Rock

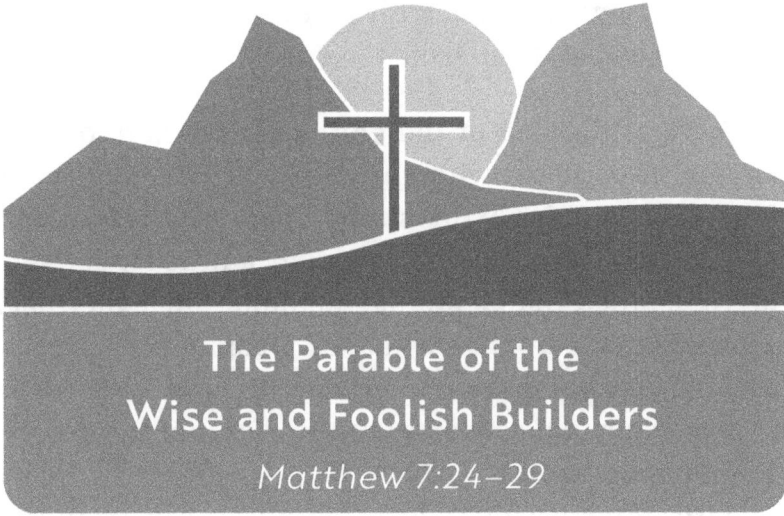

The Parable of the Wise and Foolish Builders
Matthew 7:24–29

Jesus frequently used vivid images and figurative language to capture the imagination of His listeners. Jesus lived in a time in which most information was passed on by word of mouth, and His use of these illustrations made His teaching come alive, easier to remember, and simpler to pass on to others.

Some examples of Jesus' use of such illustrations that we have seen from our study of the Sermon on the Mount include the following:

- the salt of the earth and light of the world
- a city on a hill and the lamp on a stand
- the birds of the air and lilies of the field
- a speck of dust and beam or log in a person's eye
- a father giving gifts to his children
- the narrow and wide gates
- good and bad fruit

Here at the end of the end of the Sermon on the Mount, Jesus closes with a parable. We have noticed a few other parables in this study. A parable is also a type of figurative language but is usually a little longer and more detailed than a simile, metaphor, or hyperbole. A parable is a story that makes a comparison. Jesus took His parables from everyday life and used them to teach spiritual concepts with stories that the people could understand.

Jesus often used parables to arouse curiosity in His listeners. At other times, He used parables to lead His listeners to a decision. Jesus was certainly able to heal the sick, drive out demons, and calm a storm. Yet, He could also use a simple story taken from everyday life to get people's attention and teach them lessons about spiritual truths.

The parable (7:24–27)

Jesus ended the Sermon on the Mount with a story of two men. Both built a house, but that is the only similarity between the two. The parable has been given several titles such as the Parable of the Two Houses and the Parable of the Two Builders. Perhaps, the most descriptive title is the Parable of the Wise and Foolish Builders. There is another version of this parable in Luke 6:46–49. There are few differences between the different versions of the story, but the main point is the same.

Wisdom and *foolishness* are common themes in the Bible, and a wise person is often compared with a foolish person. The book of Proverbs is filled with examples of such comparisons. Jesus also used similar examples such as the parables about the wise and foolish virgins (Matthew 25:1–13), the rich fool (Luke 12:13–21), and the shrewd or wise steward (Luke 16:1–14).

The parable is a contrast between the two builders. One was a wise man who built his house on the rock, and the other was a foolish man who built his house on the sand. Jesus was a carpenter, so this was not a hypothetical example. No doubt, Jesus had helped to build houses in the past, so this story was from everyday life and based on practical experience. Those who heard Jesus telling the story were also familiar with the situation. Choosing the right building site was important, especially in that region with extended periods of dry weather interrupted by heavy rains. A wise builder had to look ahead. A site might be smooth and level during the dry season but become a raging torrent during a flash flood.

A house built in a safe place could withstand the rain and wind, but a house built in an unsafe place could not. When the storm came, only one house remained.

The wise man took the time to carefully choose the site and build the house on a sound foundation. The foolish man failed to do this, and his house was destroyed by the storm.

There is a certain amount of symbolism in this parable. The image of a terrific storm is sometimes used, especially in the Old Testament, to depict divine judgment (Ezekiel 13:13–14; Isaiah 28:17–18). It seems likely that Jesus also included the suggestion of judgment in His parable.

The Parable of the Wise and Foolish Builders certainly connects with the contrasts found earlier in the chapter that we noted in the previous lesson, especially the wide and narrow ways. In our world, many people feel that all religions are the same. When I was a college student at a state university, I took comparative religion classes to fulfill elective requirements. The textbook used in these courses was entitled *Paths of Faith.* The basic approach of the book was that all religions worship the same deity, just by different ways and different names. Contrary to this approach, Jesus said, *"I am the way the truth and the life. No one comes to the Father except through me"* (John 14:6). There is no other way. No other god, religion, or philosophy will take His place. To build your life on the rock is to put all your trust in Jesus. There is no bargaining, no half-hearted action, only complete submission to Jesus.

Clearly, Jesus demands two things: to listen and know His words and then to follow them. Sadly, so many people may hear, but not obey the words of Jesus. Some people may want to put it off. They aren't interested in the future; there is always tomorrow. They are not like the wise man in the parable who planned ahead and built his house to withstand the storms. They are more like the foolish man who did not plan for the future, and his house was destroyed.

Some people just do not want to be inconvenienced. Being a disciple of Jesus is not convenient. It is more often demanding and, at times, difficult. Some people aren't willing to put in the effort if it is not convenient for them.

Some people simply want to "do their own thing." One of the main reasons that many people reject Christianity is because they do not want to be responsible for their actions. This was the problem of the foolish man. He did not choose the building site carefully and put the house where he wanted it.

There will be a time of testing. In the parable, it was the rain, wind, and flooding. In life, it may be illness, financial difficulties, family problems, or other challenges. For those who have not built their house on firm ground, there is bound to be trouble. Only those who have built their house on a solid foundation will be able to withstand life's storms.

The most important lesson of all from this parable is that individuals need to build their lives on the right foundation for eternity. Those who prepare themselves for God's judgment are like the man in the parable who built his house on a solid foundation. Others are like the foolish man who failed to build his house properly, and their end will be a terrible crash similar to the fate of the house built on sand.

The response of the crowds to Jesus' teaching (7:28–29)

Matthew's comments at the end of the chapter give us some idea about how the people responded to Jesus' teaching. In verse 28 we see that the people were *"amazed at his teaching."* They were astonished or dumbfounded by Jesus' words. This was because He did not teach like other teachers that they had heard. The scribes and other Jewish teachers would only appeal to some former rabbi or other authority. They did not speak for themselves as Jesus did. He spoke without any reference to authority other than his own. No one else could do this, only the incarnate Son of God.

A final thought

The Sermon on the Mount is not simply a collection of moral teachings. It is a challenge to those who enter the kingdom of God and is quite demanding. As we said at the beginning of the study, perhaps, it is best to look at the Sermon on the Mount as "ideals" for those who follow Jesus. It is unlikely that we will ever be able to follow every precept in the Sermon on the Mount, but this should not stop us from trying. If anything, Jesus' teachings found in the Sermon on the Mount should serve as "goals" for anyone who wants to be a disciple of Jesus.

Remember to keep in mind that the key to understanding the Sermon on the Mount is the word different. Jesus' disciples are to be different from those around them. Most of us do not like to stand out in the crowd, but if we are following Jesus, we will not be able to help it because we are going to be "different."

I recall the story of a minister who had spent a whole year preaching from the Sermon on the Mount. At the end of this time, he still felt that there was so much more that he had not covered. In this study, we have taken several lessons from the Sermon on the Mount, but like this minister, we have certainly not exhausted the study of this important passage. Hopefully, through this study, we have come to know more about the Sermon on the Mount and the meaning of Jesus' words for those first-century listeners as well as for us today.

PEAK REFLECTIONS

1. How does this parable relate to the narrow and wide gate and other comparisons in the last lesson?
2. What was Jesus requiring in this parable? Would you consider this to be one of the "hard sayings" of Jesus?
3. How does this parable connect with the rest of the Sermon on the Mount? How does it serve as a conclusion for the other teaching found in the Sermon on the Mount?
4. Why do so many people fail to accept Jesus and build their lives on the sand?
5. How did the crowds respond to Jesus' teaching? Why was His teaching so different?